FOR THE SWELL, SMOOTH AND DREAMY

"IN GLORIOUS TECHNICOLOR, BREATHTAKING

CINEMASCOPE AND STEREOPHONIC SOUND."

COLE PORTER, "STEREOPHONIC SOUND," 1955

Don't have a cow!

Flick Tear ass Like crazy, like wow

Blast Punch it Bug Bit Paper shaker Nosebleed

Cool Scream What's your tale,

Gig Total Knuckle sandwich Sing Sides

Cranked Submarine races Tank Cherry Make out

Hep Dig Eyeball Sounds Most Grody Baby Frosted

Kick Crazy Pound Nerd Jets What's the

Cast an eyeball Big Daddy

Passion Pit Cool it Burn rubber Hang

Wet rag Shot down Ape Real gone Stacked Split

Agitate the gravel Radioactive

Daddy-O Rag top Pad Bent eight Flip Stack up

nightingale? Cat Illuminations Tights

Kookie Fream Bread Go Ape Weed Later

Threads Fracture Wazoo Hip Fat City

Make the scene Razz my berries In orbit

buzzin', cuzzin? Back-seat bingo

Big tickle Jacketed Nest Unreal Square

Boss Clyde Flip-top

Heat Goof Word from the bird

Fireside
Fashions...

in delicious colors,
soufflé woolens
and upholstery silks

"NEW FASHION APPEAL FOR GIRLS OF ALL AGES!

An exciting, all-new kind of doll… she's shapely and grown-up… with fashion apparel authentic in every detail! This is Barbie: so curvy, flesh-toned and lifelike. Girls of all ages will thrill to the fascination of her miniature wardrobe of fine-fabric fashions: tiny zippers that really zip… jewelled earrings, necklaces and color-coordinated sun glasses!

YOU CAN
TELL
IT'S **MATTEL**
…IT'S SWELL.**"**

TEEN AGE FASHION MODEL *Barbie* ™.

Barbie ™. TEEN AGE FASHION MODE

BRYLCREEM

grooms by surface tension

Any liquid always strives to reduce its surface area when in contact with air . . . this is known as **Surface Tension** — and it is the basis on which Brylcreem works. A thin film of Brylcreem oil, together with a bland aqueous solution, coats every hair-strand and the surface tension holds the hairs together firmly but gently. Every hair is supple; every hair is lustrous. Avoid that greasy, over-oily look. Use Brylcreem, the healthy hairdressing, for the clean, smart look.

for smart, healthy hair

**LET YOUR SCALP
BREATHE . . .
ENCOURAGE YOUR
HAIR TO LIVE**

In keeping your hair and scalp healthy, Brylcreem's surface film of oil acts as a filter, which prevents micro-organisms from reaching down into the scalp. Massage with Brylcreem also frees the mouths of the follicles along which the hair grows, thus facilitating the normal flow of sebum, the scalp's natural oil. As a result, the hair is kept free from dandruff and dryness and the scalp has a chance to breathe—vitally important to the growth of strong, healthy hair. Ask for Brylcreem, the *healthy* hairdressing, in tubs 1/6, 2/3 and 4/1, or handy tubes 2/6.

BRYLCREEM®

a little dab'll do ya!®

The D.A. ("Duck's Ass") received its name from the characteristic feathered center part down the back of the head, much like the feathers of a duck's behind. The look was achieved by brushing the sides of the hair towards the center and dragging a comb down the center to part the hair in a slight wave. A generous helping of hair "grease" like Brylcreem® or even Vaseline® was required to achieve a slick style.

Variations of the D.A. were dependent on how the top of the hair was styled, as it was only the part at the nape of the neck that gave rise to the term D.A. Tony Curtis' curly-topped style was a popular variation of the smooth wave pompadour. Other variations included the bop, dupe, back sweep and crest. Whatever the style, the back was the same, and a liberal application of grease guaranteed a motionless mop.

"GOD SAVE THE QUEEN"

THE CORONATION

Elizabeth the Second, by the Grace of God,
of the United Kingdom of Great Britain and Northern Ireland
and Her other Realms and Territories Queen, Head of the Commonwealth,
Defender of the Faith.

*"I declare before you all that my whole life,
whether it be long or short, shall be devoted to your service
and the service of our great imperial family
to which we all belong."*

Daily Mirror
THE BIGGEST DAILY SALE ON EARTH

PHILIP'S KISS

I, Philip, do become your liege man of life and limb, and of earthly worship; and faith and truth I will bear unto you, to live and die, against all manner of folks. So help me God. An historic moment as the Duke of Edinburgh pays homage, then gently kisses the Queen's left cheek. The Queen and the Duke, two happy young people, are seen on the right in the golden coach.

TOMORROW
ANOTHER EXCITING PICTURE ISSUE

SPECIAL
Daily Mirror
and Sunday Pictorial
Coronation Souvenir

THE QUEEN GOES FORTH TO HER PEOPLE

Jewelled Sceptre, Orb and Crown cannot outshine the brightest jewel of all . . . Elizabeth . . . as she leaves the Abbey, indeed of England.

Daily Mirror CORONATION SOUVENIR
FORWARD WITH THE PEOPLE

HAPPY

This was the happiest picture of all

—AND GLORIOUS

ROCK around the clock

Rock Around The Clock

Shake, Rattle And Roll

Two Hound Dogs

A.B.C. Boogie

Dim, Dim The Lights

Birth Of The Boogie

BILL HALEY And His COMETS

Thirteen Women
(And Only One Man in Town)

Happy Baby

Mambo Rock

Burn That Candle

One, two, three o'clock, four o'clock, rock,
Five, six, seven o'clock, eight o'clock, rock,
Nine, ten, eleven o'clock, twelve o'clock, rock,
We're gonna ROCK around the clock tonight.
Put your glad rags on and join me, hon,
We'll have some fun when the clock strikes one,
We're gonna ROCK around the clock tonight,
We're gonna rock, rock, rock, 'til broad daylight.
We're gonna rock, gonna rock, around the clock tonight.
When the clock strikes two, three and four,
If the band slows down we'll yell for more,
We're gonna ROCK around the clock tonight,
We're gonna rock, rock, rock, 'til broad daylight.
We're gonna rock, gonna rock, around the clock tonight.
When the chimes ring five, six and seven,
We'll be right in seventh heaven.
We're gonna ROCK around the clock tonight,
We're gonna rock, rock, rock, 'til broad daylight.
We're gonna rock, gonna rock, around the clock tonight.
When it's eight, nine, ten, eleven too,
I'll be goin' strong and so will you.
We're gonna ROCK around the clock tonight,
We're gonna rock, rock, rock, 'til broad daylight.
We're gonna rock, gonna rock, around the clock tonight.
When the clock strikes twelve, we'll cool off then,
Start a rockin' round the clock again.
We're gonna ROCK around the clock tonight,
We're gonna rock, rock, rock, 'til broad daylight.
We're gonna rock, gonna rock, around the clock tonight.

Phone Booth CRAMMIN

Sometimes called **Telephone Box Squash,** there were few rules except that it was widely accepted that the booth still contained a phone. Under British rules, you had to be able to either place or receive a call, but that did not apply anywhere else. The door was left open and only half of a person needed to be inside the booth to be counted, and the booth had to be upright.

WORLD RECORD **25 people** in South Africa

"Dream as if you'll live forever. Live as if you'll die today."
James Dean

JIMMY DEAN IS NOT DEAD

The memory of this young man and of his great talent will live forever in the hearts of those who loved him

BY JIM COOK

JIMMY DEAN RETURNS

"But could there ever be only one girl in Jimmy's life? Think of the beautiful, stunning girls he was sure to meet in Hollywood!"

secret love that haunts jimmy dean

HEART THAT STALKED IN DARKNESS

The boy who refuses to DIE

James Dean Lives On . . .

Unforgotten . . . Unforgettable

"All of us were touched by Jimmy, and he was touched by greatness." *Natalie Wood*

1951   Hill Number One
1955   East of Eden
1955   **REBEL WITHOUT A CAUSE**
1956   Giant

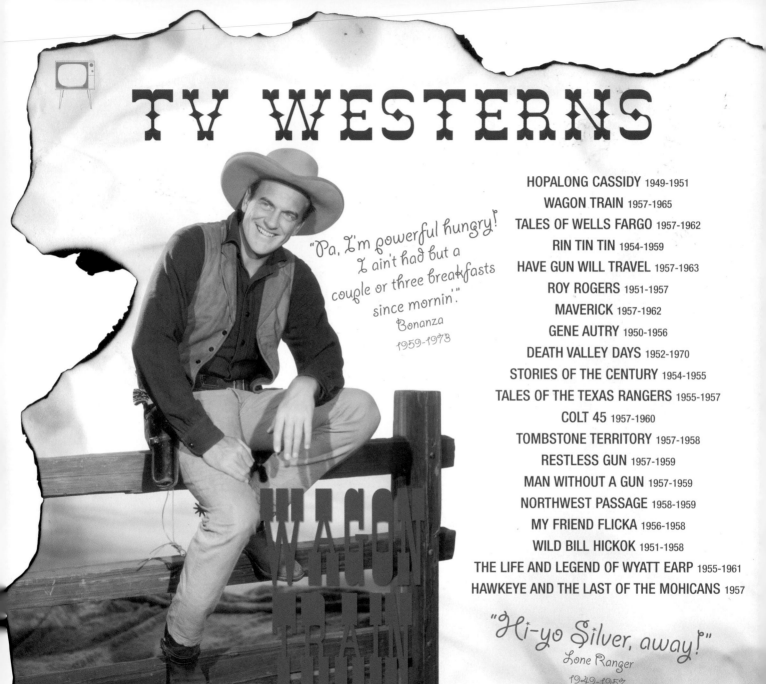

TV WESTERNS

"Pa, I'm powerful hungry!
I ain't had but a
couple or three breakfasts
since mornin'."
Bonanza
1959-1973

HOPALONG CASSIDY 1949-1951
WAGON TRAIN 1957-1965
TALES OF WELLS FARGO 1957-1962
RIN TIN TIN 1954-1959
HAVE GUN WILL TRAVEL 1957-1963
ROY ROGERS 1951-1957
MAVERICK 1957-1962
GENE AUTRY 1950-1956
DEATH VALLEY DAYS 1952-1970
STORIES OF THE CENTURY 1954-1955
TALES OF THE TEXAS RANGERS 1955-1957
COLT 45 1957-1960
TOMBSTONE TERRITORY 1957-1958
RESTLESS GUN 1957-1959
MAN WITHOUT A GUN 1957-1959
NORTHWEST PASSAGE 1958-1959
MY FRIEND FLICKA 1956-1958
WILD BILL HICKOK 1951-1958
THE LIFE AND LEGEND OF WYATT EARP 1955-1961
HAWKEYE AND THE LAST OF THE MOHICANS 1957

"Hi-yo Silver, away!"
Lone Ranger
1949-1957

WAGON TRAIN

GUNSMOKE

1955-1971

"Head 'em up, move 'em out."

Rawhide 1959-1966

TOP 10 HITS

Tutti Frutti – 1956
Long Tall Sally – 1956
Ready Teddy – 1956
Rip It Up – 1956
She's Got It – 1956
Slippin' And Slidin' – 1956
Keep A Knockin' – 1957
Jenny, Jenny – 1957
Lucille – 1957
Miss Ann – 1957
The Girl Can't Help It – 1957
Good Golly Miss Molly –1958

"A-wop-bop-
a-loo-bop
a-lop-bam-boom.
Tutti Frutti!"

LITTLE RICHARD

There wasn't anyone singing rock'n'roll when I came into it. There was no rock'n'roll. There was "Swing and Sway with Sammy Kaye." They was singing "Pennies from Heaven," but they wasn't falling in my neighborhood."

"Elvis may be the King of Rock and Roll, but I am the Queen."
Little Richard

"Rhythm and blues had a baby and somebody named it rock and roll."
Little Richard

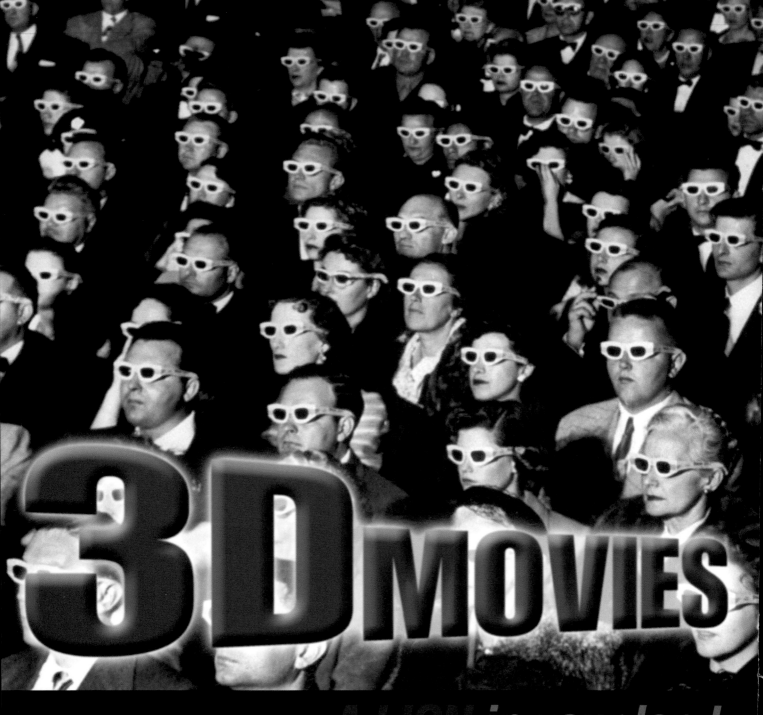

3D MOVIES

A LION in your lap !

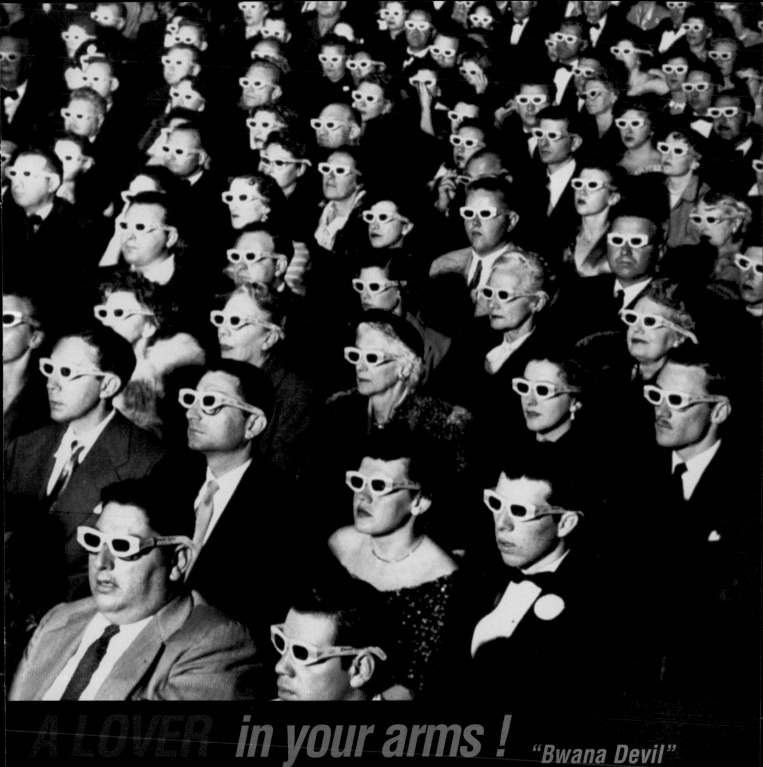

A LOVER *in your arms !* *"Bwana Devil"*

"Rock & Roll

"If your parents
don't hate it,
it ain't rock & roll."
Jim Dickinson, Producer

is a communicable disease."

New York Times, 1956

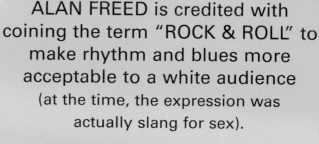

ALAN FREED is credited with coining the term "ROCK & ROLL" to make rhythm and blues more acceptable to a white audience (at the time, the expression was actually slang for sex).

On March 21, 1952, Freed was scheduled to host the "Moondog Coronation Ball" at the Cleveland Arena, but the 10,000 capacity stadium was gate-crashed by over 20,000 fans. The world's first "rock" concert had to be cancelled after only one song.

guitar wars

In 1951 FENDER® produced the first solid-body electric guitar, the "Telecaster"®.

GIBSON® launched a solid-body guitar in 1952 designed by and named for Les Paul, a legendary 1940s guitarist.

top 40 song charts

BILLBOARD MAGAZINE

Billboard Magazine premiered weekly music charts in 1955 with:

The Best Sellers in Stores
The Most Played by Jockeys
The Most Played in Juke Boxes
The Top 100.

"Sex is part of nature. I go along with nature."

> *"I am not interested in money. I just want to be wonderful."*

A TICKET TO TOMAHAWK
RIGHT CROSS
THE FIREBALL
LOVE HAPPY
THE ASPHALT JUNGLE
ALL ABOUT EVE
LOVE NEST
LET'S MAKE IT LEGAL
HOMETOWN STORY
AS YOUNG AS YOU FEEL
O. HENRY'S FULL HOUSE
MONKEY BUSINESS
CLASH BY NIGHT
WE'RE NOT MARRIED!
DON'T BOTHER TO KNOCK
NIAGARA
HOW TO MARRY A MILLIONAIRE
THERE'S NO BUSINESS LIKE SHOW BUSINESS
RIVER OF NO RETURN
THE SEVEN YEAR ITCH
BUS STOP
THE PRINCE AND THE SHOWGIRL

SOME LIKE IT HOT

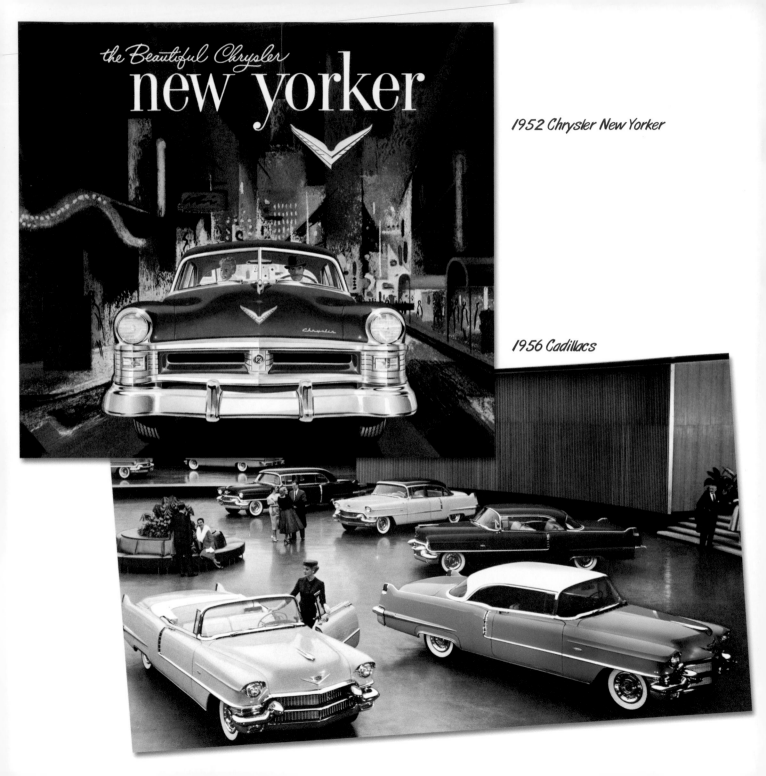

the *Beautiful Chrysler*
new yorker

1952 Chrysler New Yorker

1956 Cadillacs

1959 Mercury Colony Park
Country Cruiser

1959 Edsel Ranger

1959 EDSEL

MICKEY SPILLANE'S

MIKE HAMMER

"Crime Novels are a good way to make money."

Mickey Spillane

NOVELS from the 50s

My Gun Is Quick – 1950
Vengeance Is Mine – 1950
The Big Kill – 1951
The Long Wait – 1951
One Lonely Night –1951
Kiss Me, Deadly – 1952

MOVIES

I, The Jury – 1953
Kiss Me Deadly – 1955
My Gun Is Quick – 1957

"...but it's good garbage."

Mickey Spillane

ED MCBAIN'S

"My first contract was for three books.
I thought that might be the end of it,
easy come, easy go. The next contract was
for another three. I began to suspect that
I might be around for a while." Ed McBain

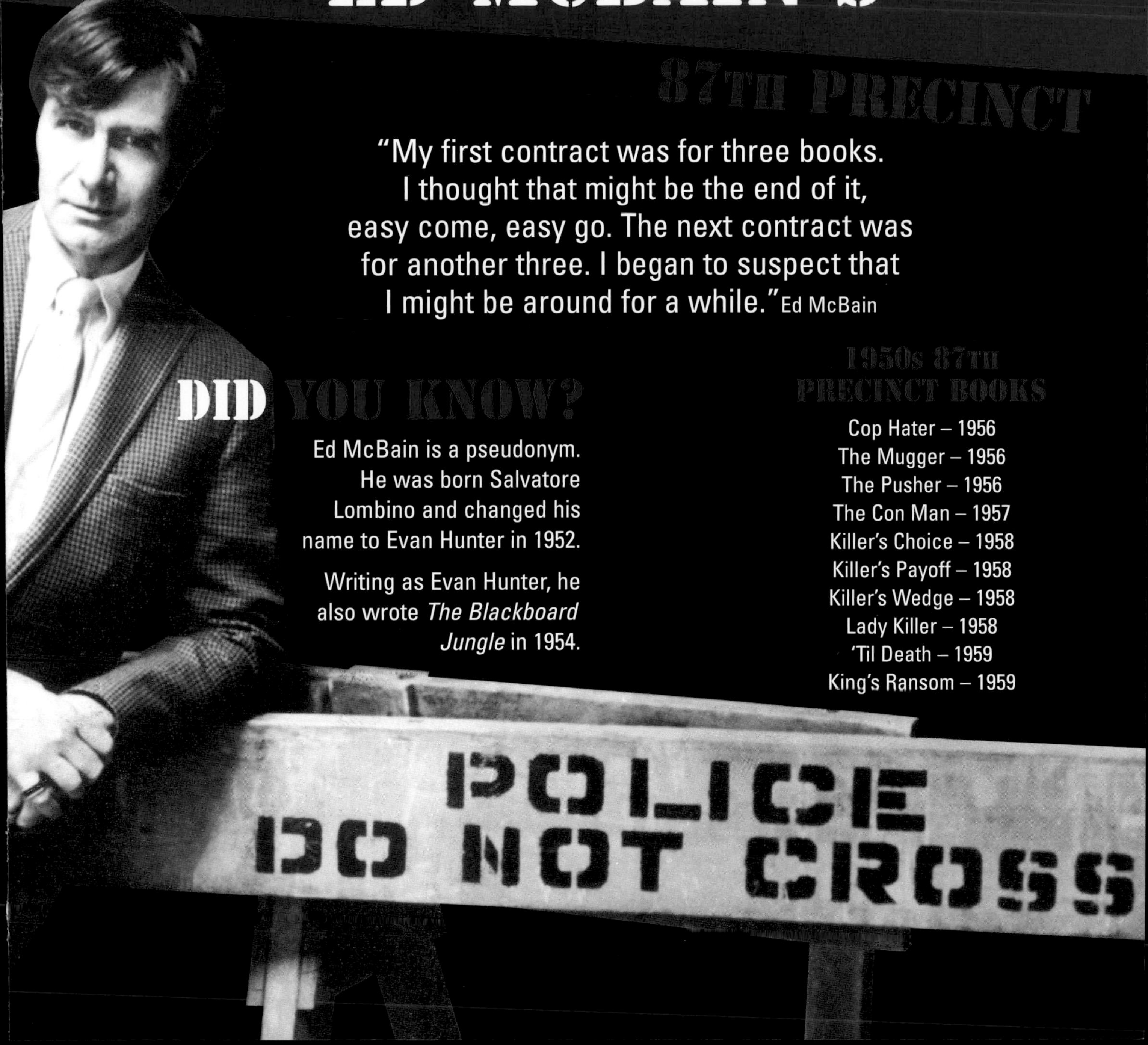

DID YOU KNOW?

Ed McBain is a pseudonym.
He was born Salvatore
Lombino and changed his
name to Evan Hunter in 1952.

Writing as Evan Hunter, he
also wrote *The Blackboard
Jungle* in 1954.

1950s 87TH PRECINCT BOOKS

Cop Hater – 1956
The Mugger – 1956
The Pusher – 1956
The Con Man – 1957
Killer's Choice – 1958
Killer's Payoff – 1958
Killer's Wedge – 1958
Lady Killer – 1958
'Til Death – 1959
King's Ransom – 1959

POLICE DO NOT CROSS

1950 – New York Yankees def. Philadelphia Phillies 4 games to 0
1951 – New York Yankees def. New York Giants 4 games to 2
1952 – New York Yankees def. Brooklyn Dodgers 4 games to 3
1953 – New York Yankees def. Brooklyn Dodgers 4 games to 2
1954 – New York Giants def. Cleveland Indians 4 games to 0
1955 – Brooklyn Dodgers def. New York Yankees 4 games to 3
1956 – New York Yankees def. Brooklyn Dodgers 4 games to 3
1957 – Milwaukee Braves def. New York Yankees 4 games to 3
1958 – New York Yankees def. Milwaukee Braves 4 games to 3
1959 – Los Angeles Dodgers def. Chicago White Sox 4 games to 2

"Yogi" Berra (real name Lawrence Peter Berra) was the backbone of the New York Yankees team for 18 seasons, and became well-known for his "Yogi-isms."

Yogi Berra

Nicknamed "The Chairman of the Board," **Whitey Ford** played for the New York Yankees as their "money pitcher." Ford has the most career wins in the history of the New York Yankees.

Whitey Ford

Charles Dillon **"Casey" Stengel** managed the New York Yankees from 1949 – 1960 winning 10 American League Championship pennants and 7 World Series'. He was the only manager to win five consecutive World Series' from 1949 – 1953.

Casey Stengel

In the 1951 National League Playoff, the Brooklyn Dodgers held a comfortable 4-1 lead over the New York Giants at the bottom of the ninth in the Game Three decider for the pennant. Then, after scoring one run and placing two men on base, the Giants' "Staten Island Scot" **Bobby Thompson** stepped up to the plate and launched Ralph Branca's pitch deep into the left field stands. It became known as "the Shot Heard 'Round the World."

The "Commerce Comet" **Micky Mantle** joined the New York Yankees in 1951. Despite numerous injuries throughout his 18-year career he finished with 536 home runs and a .298 batting average.

Bobby Thompson (center)

Mickey Mantle

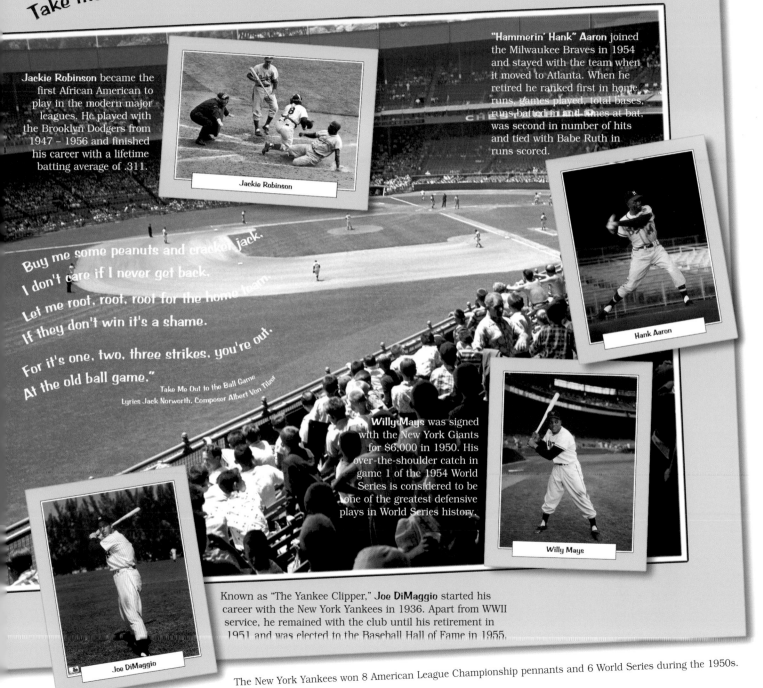

Jackie Robinson became the first African American to play in the modern major leagues. He played with the Brooklyn Dodgers from 1947 – 1956 and finished his career with a lifetime batting average of .311.

Jackie Robinson

"Hammerin' Hank" Aaron joined the Milwaukee Braves in 1954 and stayed with the team when it moved to Atlanta. When he retired he ranked first in home runs, games played, total bases, runs batted in and times at bat, was second in number of hits and tied with Babe Ruth in runs scored.

Hank Aaron

Buy me some peanuts and cracker jack.
I don't care if I never get back.
Let me root, root, root for the home team.
If they don't win it's a shame.

For it's one, two, three strikes, you're out.
At the old ball game."

Take Me Out to the Ball Game
Lyrics Jack Norworth, Composer Albert Von Tilzer

Willy Mays was signed with the New York Giants for $6,000 in 1950. His over-the-shoulder catch in game 1 of the 1954 World Series is considered to be one of the greatest defensive plays in World Series history.

Willy Mays

Known as "The Yankee Clipper," **Joe DiMaggio** started his career with the New York Yankees in 1936. Apart from WWII service, he remained with the club until his retirement in 1951 and was elected to the Baseball Hall of Fame in 1955.

Joe DiMaggio

The New York Yankees won 8 American League Championship pennants and 6 World Series during the 1950s.

"I'm singin' in the rain

I'm singin' in the rain
Just singin' in the rain
What a glorious feeling
I'm happy again
I'm laughin' at clouds
So dark up above
The sun's in my heart
And I'm ready for love
Let the stormy clouds chase
Everyone from the place
Come on with the rain
I've a smile on my face
I'll walk down the lane
With a happy refrain
Just singin'
Singin' in the rain

Dancin' in the rain
Da da da da da da…
I'm happy again…

I'm dancin'
And singin'
In the rain."

STARRING
Gene Kelly as Don Lockwood
Donald O'Connor as Cosmo Brown
Debbie Reynolds as Kathy Selden
Jean Hagen as Lina Lamont
Also featuring: Cyd Charisse, Rita Moreno

In 1953 C.A. Swanson®

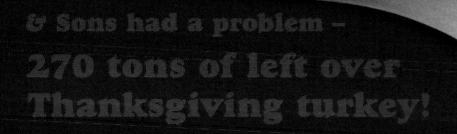

& Sons had a problem –

270 tons of left over Thanksgiving turkey!

After Thanksgiving, Swanson® had ten refrigerated railroad cars – each containing **520,000** pounds of **unsold turkeys** – going back and forth across the USA because there was nowhere to store them.

A breakthrough idea came from the trays used to serve airline food – and the TV Dinner® was born. The first production run of 5,000 dinners was filled by approximately two dozen women using ice cream scoops.

The first TV Dinner® featured turkey, corn bread dressing and gravy, buttered peas and sweet potatoes and cost 98 cents. Swanson sold **10,000,000** of them that year.

Dwight David

34th President of the United States of America

January 20, 1953 – January 20, 1961

I LIKE IKE

PEACE AND PROSPERITY WITH EISENHOWER

I STILL LIKE IKE

The Man of the Hour:

EISENHOWER

"I like Ike, you like Ike, everybody likes Ike... Let's send Ike to Washington!"

1952 television commercial, produced by Roy Disney

Eisenhower

ARMY CAREER
Assistant to General MacArthur in the Philippines, 1935 – 1939
Commander in Chief of the Allied forces in North Africa, 1942
Supreme Commander of U.S. Troops in France, D-Day, 1944
Chief of Staff, U.S. Army, 1945 – 1948
NATO Supreme Commander, 1951

"What counts is not necessarily the size of the dog in the fight – it's the size of the fight in the dog."

"In preparing for battle I have always found that plans are useless, but planning is indispensable."

"Peace and justice are two sides of the same coin."

"Only our individual faith in freedom can keep us free."

"There is nothing wrong with America that faith, love of freedom, intelligence, and energy of her citizens cannot cure."

Dreamy!

Christmas morning she'll be happier with a Hoover

Handy hints for Christmas Presents!

Doris

Films

Young Man with a Horn (1950)
Tea for Two (1950)
The West Point Story (1950)
Storm Warning (1951)
Lullaby of Broadway (1951)
On Moonlight Bay (1951)
See You in My Dreams (1951)
Starlift (1951)
The Winning Team (1952)
April in Paris (1952)
By the Light of the Silvery Moon (1953)
Calamity Jane (1953)
Young at Heart (1954)
Love Me or Leave Me (1955)
The Man Who Knew Too Much (1956)
Julie (1956)
The Pajama Game (1957)
Teacher's Pet (1958)
The Tunnel of Love (1958)
It Happened to Jane (1959)
Pillow Talk (1959)

"The Cutest

Day

Blonde of Them All."

Que Sera Sera

When I was just a little girl,
I asked my mother, "What will I be?
Will I be pretty? Will I be rich?"
Here's what she said to me:

"Que sera, sera,
Whatever will be, will be;
The future's not ours to see.
Que sera, sera,
What will be, will be."

When I was just a child in school,
I asked my teacher, "What will I try?
Should I paint pictures? Should I sing songs?"
This was her wise reply:

chorus

When I grew up and fell in love.
I asked my sweetheart, "What lies ahead?
Will we have rainbows? Day after day?"
Here's what my sweetheart said:

chorus

Now I have children of my own.
They ask their mother, "What will I be?
Will I be handsome? Will I be rich?"
I tell them tenderly:

chorus

"Que Sera, Sera!"

From *The Man Who Knew Too Much*
starring Doris Day and James Stewart.
Written by Jay Livingston and Ray Evans.

How to stay cool when the heat's on.

Sizzling-good eating,
outdoor style.

3 MINUTES, **59.4** SECONDS!

"Well, it is all right, this running business, but I hope it doesn't distract you from your work as a medical student."

Mrs Bannister (Roger's mother)

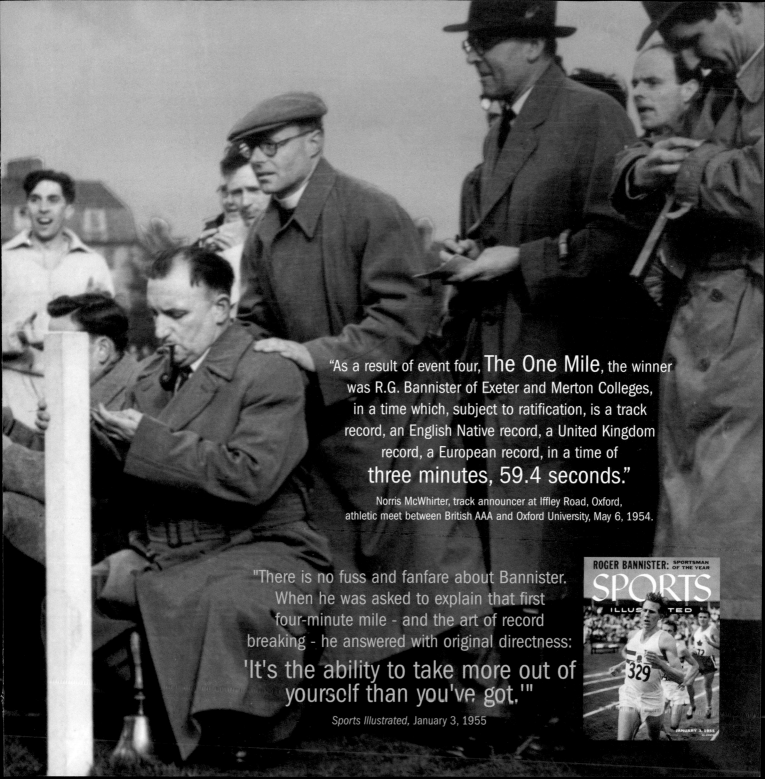

"As a result of event four, The One Mile, the winner was R.G. Bannister of Exeter and Merton Colleges, in a time which, subject to ratification, is a track record, an English Native record, a United Kingdom record, a European record, in a time of **three minutes, 59.4 seconds.**"

Norris McWhirter, track announcer at Iffley Road, Oxford, athletic meet between British AAA and Oxford University, May 6, 1954.

"There is no fuss and fanfare about Bannister. When he was asked to explain that first four-minute mile - and the art of record breaking - he answered with original directness: **'It's the ability to take more out of yourself than you've got.'**"

Sports Illustrated, January 3, 1955

ROGER BANNISTER: SPORTSMAN OF THE YEAR
SPORTS
ILLUSTRATED
329
JANUARY 3, 1955

AMERICAN BANDSTAND®

Originally hosted by Bob Horn and called **"Bob Horn's Bandstand"** the show commenced on October 7, 1952.

In 1956 the show was picked up by ABC and was renamed with new host Dick Clark.

By 1959 the audience was **20 million viewers.**

DID YOU KNOW?

The first song played when the show first aired nationally was "Whole Lotta Shaking Goin' On" by Jerry Lee Lewis.

Elvis Presley never appeared.

BB King was the only singer NOT to lip-synch.

In 1957, two schoolboys who called themselves Tom and Jerry made their debut singing their own song, "Hey Schoolgirl." They would later become known as Simon and Garfunkel.

"The Regulars" — also known as "The Committee" — were local dancers who appeared on the show each week. They received 15,000 fan letters a week, and were credited with inventing a number of dance crazes including *"The Hop,"* *"The Stroll,"* *"The Circle"* and *"The Chalypso."*

The Hop

The dance couples were:

Arlene Sullivan and Kenny Rossi

Bunny Gibson and Ed Kelly

Joyce Shafer and Norman Kerr

Carole Scaldeferri and Nick Gaeta

Mary Beltrante and Lou DeSero

Barbara Levick and Joe Wissert

Janet Hamill and Eddie Connor

Carmen Jimenez and Frank Vacca

Dottie Horner and Frank Spagnuola

Frani Giordano and Mike Balera.

Operation Cue, the Federal
Civil Defense Administration's
atomic test program, finds

"frozen food is safe to eat
and retains its flavor
and frozen state despite
radiation exposure!"

introducing...

1950

KRAFT® Deluxe Processed Cheese

MINUTE® Rice

The Open Kettle in Massachusetts is renamed Dunkin' Donuts®

The Kenwood Chef food processor

1951

Sugar Pops® cereal

Jack-in-the Box® opens in San Diego

Swanson® beef, chicken, turkey pot pies

Tropicana® juice

Duncan Hines® cake mix

1952

Pream powdered non-dairy coffee creamer

Kelloggs® Sugar Smacks® & Sugar Frosted Flakes®

Teabags

Birds Eye® frozen peas

Colonel Sanders sells first Kentucky Fried Chicken franchise

Lipton® onion soup mix

Mrs. Paul's® fish sticks

No-Cal Beverage gingerale by Kirsch

1953

Saran™ Wrap

KRAFT® Cheez Whiz

Eggo® frozen waffles

1954

M&M® peanut chocolate candies

Swanson TV Dinners®

First Burger King® opens in Miami

KRAFT® Cracker Barrel® cheese

Trix® by General Mills

Reddi-wip®

Wake up to TANG!

More vitamin C than orange juice!

"The modern woman owes a lot to today's good sense in diet. She eats light, drinks light, and keeps her youthful figure longer. She looks better, feels better. Men like her better. And so does her insurance company." Pepsi-Cola, 1953

1955

Kelloggs® introduces Tony the Tiger®

Quaker® Oats Instant Oatmeal

First McDonald's™ opens in Illinois

Campbell's® Soup Green Bean Bake

Kelloggs® Special K® cereal

KRAFT® Processed Cheese

Birds Eye® fish fingers (UK)

Frozen pizza

The first microwave oven for home use

1956

Certs® candy breath mint

The electric can opener

1957

Tang® breakfast beverage

Better Homes & Gardens® first microwave cooking article

Margarine sales overtake butter sales

Burger King's® The Whopper®

1958

The Jolly Green Giant® first TV commercial

First Pizza Hut® opens in Kansas

Sweet'n'Low® artificial sweetener

Rice-a-Roni®

Kelloggs® Cocoa Krispies®

General Mills Cocoa Puffs®

Aluminum beverage cans

Tater Tots®

1959

Hawaiian Punch®

Danny's Coffee Shops are renamed Denny's®

Häagen-Dazs® ice cream

General Mills Frosty O's®

Teflon® coated pots and pans

COUNTRY

HANK WILLIAMS
(No. 1 singles)

"Long Gone Lonesome Blues" – 1950

"Why Don't You Love Me?"– 1950

"Moanin' The Blues" – 1950

"Cold, Cold Heart" – 1951

"Hey, Good Lookin'" – 1951

"Jambalaya" – 1952

"Kaw-Liga" – 1952

"Take These Chains From My Heart" – 1952

"Your Cheatin' Heart" – 1953

"I'll Never Get Out of This World Alive" – 1953

PATSY CLINE

"Come on In" – 1956

"Walkin' After Midnight" – 1957

THE GRAND OLE OPRY®

"The Grand Ole Opry"® is the world's longest running live radio program broadcasting on WSM radio every Saturday night since November 28, 1925. By the 1950s, its audience was an estimated 10 million people.

Roy Acuff was a regular performer on "The Grand Ole Opry"® and his music publishing venture, Rose-Acuff, first signed the singing talents of Hank Williams, The Everly Brothers and Roy Orbison.

GENE AUTRY

"Peter Cottontail" – 1950

"Frosty The Snowman" – 1950

TEX RITTER

"Do Not Forsake Me" from the movie High Noon – 1952

introducing...

1950
KRAFT® Deluxe Processed Cheese

MINUTE® Rice

The Open Kettle in Massachusetts is renamed Dunkin' Donuts®

The Kenwood Chef food processor

1951
Sugar Pops® cereal

Jack-in-the Box® opens in San Diego

Swanson® beef, chicken, turkey pot pies

Tropicana® juice

Duncan Hines® cake mix

1952
Pream powdered non-dairy coffee creamer

Kelloggs® Sugar Smacks® & Sugar Frosted Flakes®

Teabags

Birds Eye® frozen peas

Colonel Sanders sells first Kentucky Fried Chicken franchise

Lipton® onion soup mix

Mrs. Paul's® fish sticks

No-Cal Beverage gingerale by Kirsch

1953
Saran™ Wrap

KRAFT® Cheez Whiz

Eggo® frozen waffles

1954
M&M® peanut chocolate candies

Swanson TV Dinners®

First Burger King® opens In Miami

KRAFT® Cracker Barrel® cheese

Trix® by General Mills

Reddi-wip®

Wake up to TANG!

More vitamin C than orange juice!

"The modern woman owes a lot to today's good sense in diet. She eats light, drinks light, and keeps her youthful figure longer. She looks better, feels better. Men like her better. And so does her insurance company." Pepsi-Cola, 1953

1955
Kelloggs® introduces Tony the Tiger®

Quaker® Oats Instant Oatmeal

First McDonald's™ opens in Illinois

Campbell's® Soup Green Bean Bake

Kelloggs® Special K® cereal

KRAFT® Processed Cheese

Birds Eye® fish fingers (UK)

Frozen pizza

The first microwave oven for home use

1956
Certs® candy breath mint

The electric can opener

1957
Tang® breakfast beverage

Better Homes & Gardens® first microwave cooking article

Margarine sales overtake butter sales

Burger King's® The Whopper®

1958
The Jolly Green Giant® first TV commercial

First Pizza Hut® opens in Kansas

Sweet'n'Low® artificial sweetener

Rice-a-Roni®

Kelloggs® Cocoa Krispies®

General Mills Cocoa Puffs®

Aluminum beverage cans

Tater Tots®

1959
Hawaiian Punch®

Danny's Coffee Shops are renamed Denny's®

Häagen-Dazs® ice cream

General Mills Frosty O's®

Teflon® coated pots and pans

COUNTRY

HANK WILLIAMS
(No. 1 singles)

"Long Gone Lonesome Blues" – 1950

"Why Don't You Love Me?" – 1950

"Moanin' The Blues" – 1950

"Cold, Cold Heart" – 1951

"Hey, Good Lookin" – 1951

"Jambalaya" – 1952

"Kaw-Liga" – 1952

"Take These Chains From My Heart" – 1952

"Your Cheatin' Heart" – 1953

"I'll Never Get Out of This World Alive" – 1953

PATSY CLINE

"Come on In" – 1956

"Walkin' After Midnight" – 1957

THE GRAND OLE OPRY®

"The Grand Ole Opry"® is the world's longest running live radio program broadcasting on WSM radio every Saturday night since November 28, 1925. By the 1950s, its audience was an estimated 10 million people.

Roy Acuff was a regular performer on "The Grand Ole Opry"® and his music publishing venture, Rose-Acuff, first signed the singing talents of Hank Williams, The Everly Brothers and Roy Orbison.

GENE AUTRY

"Peter Cottontail" – 1950

"Frosty The Snowman" – 1950

TEX RITTER

"Do Not Forsake Me" from the movie *High Noon* – 1952

MUSIC

The Louisiana Hayride

"The Louisiana Hayride" was a performance arena and radio show broadcast on KWKH from the Municipal Auditorium in Shreveport, Louisiana. In March 1959 the admission fee was $1 for adults and 50 cents for children. Many country and western stars began their careers at the "Hayride" before moving to the "Grand Ole Opry"® as they became more successful.

Slim Whitman joined the "Hayride" on April 7, 1950. His 1950 song, "Indian Love Call," reached the top of the country chart.

Jim Reeves came to KWKH as an announcer in December 1952. When Hank Williams didn't show up to play, Reeves filled in and was a hit – his song "Mexican Joe" topped the country chart.

Elvis Presley appeared on the "Hayride" in October 1954, having first approached "The Grand Ole Opry"® and been turned down. He originally earned $18 per show but for his final performance three years later, the show had to move from its 3,200 seat auditorium to the State Fairgrounds which had a capacity of 10,000 people.

It was "One of the finest displays of mass hysteria in Shreveport history" according to the report in the following day's *Shreveport Times*. The phrase

"Elvis has left the building"

was credited to producer Horace Logan in 1956 it was his attempt to quiet the frenzied audience at the end of Elvis's last appearance.

JIM REEVES
Host of The Louisiana Hayride

"*Mexican Joe*" – 1953
"*Bimbo*" – 1953
"*Yonder Comes a Sucker*" – 1955
"*Four Walls*" – 1957
"*Blue Boy*" – 1958
"*He'll Have To Go*" – 1959

SLIM WHITMAN

"*Indian Love Call*" – 1950

Johnny Cash and the Tennessee Two first appeared on the "Hayride" on December 3, 1953.

JOHNNY CASH

"*Hey Porter*" – 1955
"*Cry, Cry, Cry*" – 1955
"*I Walk The Line*" – 1958
"*Don't Take Your Guns To Town*" – 1958

"Say, Kids, what time is it?"
"It's Howdy Doody Time"

"who's the leader of the club That's made for you and me?
M-I-C-K-E-Y
M-O-U-S-E!"

Howdy Doody
1947 – 1960

"It's Howdy Doody Time
It's Howdy Doody Time
Bob Smith and Howdy Doo
Say Howdy Doo to you."

Original Mouseketeers

Sharon Baird
Bobby Burgess
Lonnie Burr
Tommy Cole
Annette Funicello
Darlene Gillespie
Cubby O'Brien
Karen Pendelton
Doreen Tracey

ANNETTE

JIMMI

"Lassie, come here girl!"

Captain Kangaroo
1955 – 1984

Lassie
1954 – 1957
Tommy Rettig as Jeff Miller

1957 – 1964
Jon Provost
as Timmy Martin

Mickey
Mouse
Club
1955 – 1958

CHERYL

DARLENE

TOMMY

SHARON

SHERRY

CUBBY

Captain
Kangaroo
played by Bob Keeshan
"Featuring Tom
Terrific and his
Sidekick, Mighty Manfred
the Wonder Dog!"

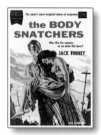

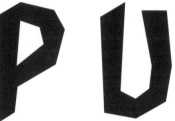

PULP

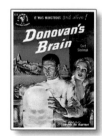
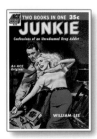

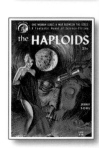

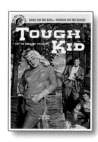

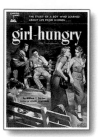

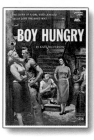

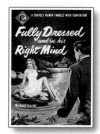

FICTION

"Anyone alive who had a TV felt that Lucy was part of the family."

Carol Burnett

"I love Lucy and she loves me
We're as happy as two can be
Sometimes we quarrel but then
How we love making up again
Lucy kisses like no one can
She's my Mrs. and I'm her man
And life is heaven you see
Cause I love Lucy
Yes I love Lucy
And Lucy loves me!"

DANGER
BE CAREFUL
WHEN BELT
IS IN MOTION.

"I Love Lucy"

Premiered 9:00PM October 15, 1951

Ethel: "I refuse to go to the theater with anyone who thinks I'm a hippopotamus!"

Ricky: "Did you call her that?"

Lucy: "No!"

Ethel: "Ha!"

Lucy: "All I did was intimate that she was a little hippy. But on second glance she has got the biggest pottamus I've ever seen."

"Waaaaaaah!"

"Lucy, I'm home."

"The secret of staying young is live honestly, eat slowly, and lie about your age."

Lucy: Hello friends, I'm your Vitameatavegamin girl. Are you tired, rundown, listless? Do you poop out at parties? Are you unpopular?

The answer to all your problems is in this little bottle. Vitameatavegamin. Vitameatavegamin contains vitamins, meat, vegetables and minerals. Yes, with Vitameatavegamin you can spoon your way to health. All you do is take a tablespoon after every meal. It's so tasty too, it's just like candy. So, why don't you join the thousands of happy, peppy people and get a great big bottle of Vitameatavegamin. That's Vita-meata-vegamin.

3... 2... 1...

"In spite of the opinions of certain narrow-minded people who would shut up the human race upon this globe, we shall one day travel to the moon, the planets, and the stars with the same facility, rapidity and certainty as we now make the ocean voyage from Liverpool to New York."
Jules Verne

October 4, 1957 – the USSR launches Sputnik 1, which becomes the first satellite to orbit the Earth.

February 1, 1958 – the USA launches the first US satellite, Explorer 1, and discovers The Van Allen radiation belt around the Earth during the mission.

August 20, 1953 – The U.S. Army launches its first Medium Range Ballistic Missile, the *Redstone Rocket.*

November 3, 1957 – the Soviet Union launches Sputnik 2 with "Laika" on board, a female part-Samoyed terrier dog. It re-enters the Earth's atmosphere on April 14, 1958 after 162 days in orbit.

BLAST-OFF!

January 2, 1959 – the Soviet Union launches the first lunar probe, Luna 1, which passes within 6,000 kilometers of the moon. September 12, 1959 – Luna 2 launches and strikes the moon two days later – the first man-made object to connect with another celestial body. Luna 3 follows October 4, 1959, and takes the first photograph of the moon's far side.

"Space travel is bunk."
Sir Harold Spencer Jones, Astronomer Royal, UK, 1957, two weeks before Sputnik orbited the earth.

July 29, 1958 – US Congress passes the "Aeronautics and Space Act" creating the National Aeronautics and Space Administration (NASA).

"Amtico Rubber Flooring.

Springy underfoot as a golf green…"

Amtico Rubber Flooring, 1951

"There's a world of aluminum in the wonderful world of tomorrow… where you and your young will take your ease in gay-hued chairs made of light, strong, carefree aluminum…"

Alcoa Aluminum, 1950

brand new and beautiful aristocrats

M A R T E X

Kitchen Linens
…100% pure Irish linen

Time-savers all, they're the gayest collection of towels that ever decked your kitchen. And so irresistibly pretty, you'll want to convert them into cocktail aprons, place mats, tray cloths, and gifts for all your friends. Loomed by Martex right here in the U.S.A. these fine Irish linen towels will do the very best job on your dishes. 17" x 30", $1.29 each, at stores listed. Martex, 65 Worth St., New York 13.

Breakfast TIME   *Tea* TIME   *Party* TIME

"New living ideas: modern *classics* with *perfectly* washable *Fiberglas.*"

Fiberglas drapes, 1958

"It's so beautiful you can't stop looking at it… yet so automatic it cooks a complete meal without a glance from you."

American Gas Association, 1950

"**The Decorator Refrigerator!**
Revolutionary new idea enables you to make your refrigerator a feature of your kitchen decoration. Match it with your curtains… And you can change it as often as you change your mind!"

International Harvester Decorator Refrigerator, 1953

Richard Sherman: *"There's gin and vermouth. That's a Martini."*

The Girl (Marilyn Monroe): *"Oh, that sounds cool! I think I'll have a glass of that – a big tall one!"*
The Seven Year Itch, 1955

"Come fly with me, let's fly, let's fly away
If you could use some exotic booze
There's a bar in far Bombay
Come fly with me, let's fly, let's fly away."

Frank Sinatra, "Come Fly with Me"

Classic 50s Cocktails

Martini
Vodkatini
Whiskey Sour
Manhattan
Gimlet
Tom Collins
Mai Tai
Singapore Sling
Mojito
Sidecar

ESSENTIAL COCKTAIL EQUIPMENT

Stainless steel cocktail shaker
Cocktail glassware
Olives
Lemon twists
Cocktail onions
Cocktail toothpicks
(with curly cellophane)
Cocktail umbrellas
Ice
Spirit measure or jigger

THE VODKATINI

Introduced by Jerome Zerbe, Society Editor of *Town and Country* Magazine, in 1951

**3 parts Vodka
1 part Dry Vermouth**

In an ice-filled shaker, pour in Vodka and Vermouth and shake. Strain into chilled Martini glass and garnish with a green olive or a lemon twist.

Alice and Jerry

The Alice and Jerry Reading Program, written by Mabel O'Donnell and Alice Carey and illustrated by Margaret and Florence Hoopes, was first published in the USA in 1936

by Row, Peterson and Company and was a popular reading program in schools in the 1940s and 1950s.

Dick and Jane

The Sally, Dick and Jane "Curriculum Foundation Series," designed primarily by Dr. William S. Gray and William H. Elson and illustrated by Eleanor Campbell, was first published in the USA by Scott, Foresman and Company in 1930.

Janet and John

In other parts of the world Alice and Jerry were called Janet and John. Using Margaret and Florence Hoopes illustrations, New Zealander Rona Munro wrote new text and Janet and John taught British, Australian and New Zealand children to read from the 1950s through the 1970s.

Spot run!"

Featuring Dick, Jane, Sally, Spot, Puff, Tim, Pam and Penny it was one of the first integrated learning programs and was widely used throughout the 1940s and 1950s.

GOLF

BEN HOGAN

"The Hawk"
Ben Hogan won 63 professional golf tournaments and is one of only five players to have won golf's Grand Slam: The Masters, US Open, British Open and the USPGA Championship.

Ben Hogan suffered a near-fatal car crash in 1949, and was told he may never walk again. He went on to tie with Sam Snead in the 1950 Los Angeles Open, losing in an 18-hole playoff and won his second US Open five months later.

CAREER (1950s):

1950 – US Open

1950 – "Player of the Year"

1951 – Masters

1951 – US Open

1953 – Masters

1953 – US Open

1953 – The Open Championship

SAM SNEAD

"Slammin' Sam"
Sam Snead won 81 American golf tournaments – the only title he missed out on was the US Open. In 1950, Snead won 11 events on the PGA Tour, including an 18-hole playoff with Ben Hogan to win the Los Angeles Open.

CAREER (1950s):

1951 – USPGA Championship

1952 – Masters

1954 – Masters

"The only reason I ever played golf in the first place was so I could afford to hunt and fish."

MILDRED "Babe" DIDRIKSON ZAHARIAS

Babe took up golf in 1933 and turned professional in 1947 after spending nine years battling to have her amateur status confirmed. She won 82 golf tournaments (both amateur and professional) in her career and during the 1946 – 1947 seasons won 17 tournaments in a row. She twice qualified for the Los Angeles Open (a men's tournament).

In 1950, Babe completed the Grand Slam of the LPGA, winning the US Open, The Titleholders and the Western Open, as well as being the leading money-earner on the Tour.

Babe was one of 14 founding players, along with Patty Berg and Louise Suggs, of The Ladies Professional Golf Association (LPGA) established in 1950.

1950s TITLES
1950 – US Women's Open
1950 – Titleholders
1950 – The Western Open
1952 – Titleholders
1954 – US Women's Open

"All of my life I've always had the urge to do things better than anybody else."

ARNOLD PALMER

Arnold Palmer made his professional debut at the Miami Open in Florida in 1954.

His first professional win was at the Canadian Open in 1955. He was the first golfer to win the Masters four times, win $1 million in prize money and to travel the world in his own private jet.

"Arnie's Army" was the moniker given to the legion of fans who turned up at the greens to follow their hero.

CAREER (1950s):
1954 – US Amateur
1955 – Canadian Open
1958 – Masters

"I have a tip that can take 5 strokes off anyone's golf game. It's called an eraser."

It's So Easy, Peggy Sue, Wishing, That'll Be The Day, Everyday,
Heartbeat, It Doesn't Matter Anymore, Maybe Baby, Raining In My
Heart, Rave On, Well All Right, Waiting, Hoping, Blue Days
Black Nights, Oh Boy, Got Me Blues, Changing All Those
Changes, Don't Come Back, Down The Line, Early In The
Morning, Baby Come Out To, Gonna Love You To, I'm Gonna
Set My Foot Down, I'm Looking Someone To Love, Love Me, You're
The One, That's My Desire, Ways, Wait Till Sunshines Nellie
You've Got Love, What They Say, Words Of Love
You're The One, What To Do, Ting A Ling, That
Makes It Tough, Cafe, Slippin' And Sliddin'
Rock A, Round With Ollie Vee, Ready
Teddy, My Heart, Stay Close To Me
Fools Paradise, Love Is Strange, It's Not My
Fault, It's Love, Little Baby, Lonesome
Tears, Got You, Been Lonely,
Guess That I Was Just, Modern Don Juan
Midnight Shift, Now, dreams, Queen Of The
Ballroom, Look At Me, Turning The Game, Brown
Eyed A Handsome Man, Let's Play House, Down
The Line, Dearest, Down Heart, Baby It's Love,
An Empty Cup, Because Baby Won't You Come

THE DAY THE MUSIC DIED

"In England Buddy Holly was as big as Elvis. Everything that came out was a record smash number one. By about 1958 it was either Elvis or Buddy Holly. It was split into two camps. The Elvis fans were the heavy leather boys and the Buddy Holly ones all somehow looked like Buddy Holly. Buddy Holly was the start of everything. His music had it all." KEITH RICHARDS.

Tuesday, February 3, 1959

LUBBOCK ROCK 'N' ROLL STAR KILLED

Buddy Holly, Three others In Air Crash. Ritchie Valens, J.P. Richardson, Pilot Also Dead. Buddy Holly, 22-year-old Lubbock rock 'n' roll singing star, was killed along with three other men in the crash of a light chartered plane northwest of Mason City, Iowa, this morning, the Associated Press reported.

Two of the other victims, Ritchie Valens, 21, Los Angeles, and J.P. "Big Bopper" Richardson, Beaumont, also were nationally known rock 'n' roll singers.

The birth of the credit card

"Buddy, could you spare a cup of coffee until I can get to a Diners' Club restaurant?"

"*Charge it*"

Say "**CHARGE IT**" for...
FOOD · DRINKS · ENTERTAINMENT
HOTEL ACCOMMODATIONS
PACKAGE LIQUORS · FLOWERS · GIFTS

Auto rentals through
HERTZ RENT-A-CAR

Motel service through
CONGRESS OF MOTOR HOTELS

Liquor gifts through
BEVERAGE GIFT SERVICE

Your Credit is good
wherever you go
AS A MEMBER OF THE *Diners' c*

EXPIRES **MAY 31, 1958**
SUBJECT TO TERMS ON REVERSE SIDE

NOT VALID OUTSIDE

EXPIRES **SEPTEMBER 30, 1957**
SUBJECT TO TERMS ON REVERSE SIDE

the *Diners' Club*
CREDIT
IDENTIFICATION
CARD
SPECIMEN
YOUR ACCOUNT NO.

Winsted Evening Citizen
CASH DIED TODAY

"... in February 1950, Frank McNamara and his partner, Ralph Schneider, dined at Major's Cabin Grill.
When the bill came McNamara presented a small, cardboard card
- *a Diners Club Card* -
and signed for the purchase. In the credit card industry, this event is known as the First Supper."

Opening Day Attractions

July 17, 1955

Main Street U.S.A

The Santa Fe and Disneyland® Railroad
Main Street Cinema
Horse-Drawn Street Cars
Horse-Drawn Fire Wagon
Horse-Drawn Surreys
Main Street Penny Arcade

Adventureland

The Jungle Cruise

Frontierland

The Mark Twain Steamboat
Stage Coaches
The Golden Horseshoe Review
Mule Pack

Fantasyland

King Arthur Carousel
Peter Pan's Flight
Snow White's Scary Adventures
Mad Tea Party
Canal Boats of the World
Mr. Toad's Wild Ride

Tomorrowland

Space Station X-1
Autopia
Circarama

the happiest place on earth

"Disneyland will never be completed.

It will continue to grow as long as there is imagination left in the world."

WALT DISNEY

Davy CROCKETT

**"BORN ON A MOUNTAINTOP IN TENNESSEE,
GREENEST STATE IN THE LAND OF THE FREE,
RAISED IN THE WOODS SO HE KNEW EVERY TREE,
KILT HIM A B'AR WHEN HE WAS ONLY 3…**

"We had no idea what was going to happen on Crockett. Why, by the time the first show finally got on the air, we were already shooting the third one and calmly killing Davy off at the Alamo. It became one of the biggest over-night hits in TV history, and there we were with just three films and a dead hero!"
Walt Disney.

DAVY CROCKETT INDIAN FIGHTER (Dec 1954)
DAVY CROCKETT GOES TO CONGRESS (Jan 1955)
DAVY CROCKETT AT THE ALAMO (Feb 1955)
DAVY CROCKETT'S KEELBOAT RACES (Nov 1955)
DAVY CROCKETT AND THE ROVER PIRATES (Dec 1955)
Starring **FESS PARKER**

"Which will be exhausted first; the supply of raccoons or the parents who have to buy the caps?" *Life* magazine

$300 million worth of coonskin caps and Davy Crockett accessories were sold between 1954 and 1955.

DAVY, DAVY CROCKETT, KING OF THE WILD FRONTIER!"

"THE BALLAD OF DAVY CROCKETT"

Elvis the Pelvis

"Some people tap their feet, some people snap their fingers, and some people sway back and forth. I just sorta do 'em all together, I guess."

The King!

"There is
NO reason
anyone would
want a computer
in their home."

Ken Olson, President,
Chairman and Founder,
Digital Equipment Corp.

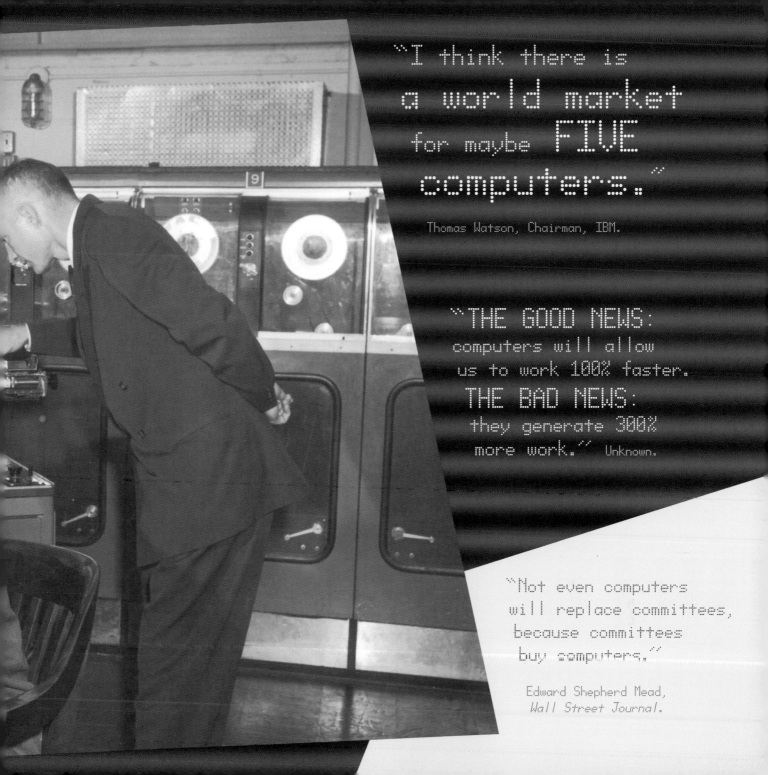

"I think there is
a world market
for maybe FIVE
computers."

Thomas Watson, Chairman, IBM.

"THE GOOD NEWS:
computers will allow
us to work 100% faster.
THE BAD NEWS:
they generate 300%
more work." Unknown.

"Not even computers
will replace committees,
because committees
buy computers."

Edward Shepherd Mead,
Wall Street Journal.

Lingerie

"The Foundation is Fit

Today brassieres are made in a large variety of fittings, allowing for the width of the back and depth of the chest as well as the size of the bust. The bust should be brought forward from beneath the armpits, yet a good division still maintained."

I dreamed I posed for a Fashion Ad
in my *maidenform* bra

"Caring for a Girdle
Wash them frequently

This is the first and most important rule in taking care of any foundation garment."

Good Housekeeping Magazine, November 1954

we sell this dream

Jantzen

you'll never know until you try

CURVALINE
by *Jantzen*

Ben Hur was one of the first films to involve big marketing tie-ins, including hundreds of toys as well as "Ben-His" and "Ben-Hers" towels.

The film grossed in excess of $76 million, and cost $19 million to make.

BIGGER THAN

It took 6 years to prepare the film shoot, with over 6 months on-location work in Italy. The movie featured more crew and extras than any other film before it.

The Chariot race arena took up 18 acres and was one of the most expensive sets ever constructed, using 1 million feet of wood, 250 miles of metal tubing, 1 million pounds of plaster and 40,000 tons of sand from nearby beaches.

The chariot race sequence alone cost $1 million, took three months to shoot and used 8,000 extras.

There were more
than 300 sets covering
148 acres – most at
Cinecitta Studios in Rome.

BEN HUR!"

Ben Hur won 11 of the
12 Academy Awards® it
was nominated for.

Best Actor; Best Actor in a Supporting Role;
Best Art Direction-Set Decoration, Color;Best
Cinematography, Color; Best Costume
Design, Color; Best Director; Best Effects,
Special Effects; Best Film Editing; Best Music,
Scoring of a Dramatic or Comedy Picture;
Best Picture; Best Sound.

The movie was filmed in Camera
65, a wide-screen process using
film 65mm wide. The cameras cost
$100,000 each.

J.R.R. TOLKIEN

The Lord of the Rings: The Fellowship of the Ring published July 1954

The Lord of the Rings: The Two Towers published November 1954

The Lord of the Rings: The Return of the King published October 1955

The first print run of The Fellowship of the Ring sold out within a month. By the time The Two Towers was released, The Fellowship of the Ring was on its fourth reprint and The Two Towers reprinted twice in 1955 alone.

"**I am in fact a hobbit (in all but size).**
I like gardens, trees and unmechanized farmlands; I smoke a pipe, and like good plain food (unrefrigerated). I like, and even dare to wear in these dull days, ornamental waistcoats. I am fond of mushrooms (out of a field); have a very simple sense of humor (which even my appreciative critics find tiresome); I go to bed late (when possible). I do not travel much."

J.R.R. TOLKIEN, 1958

THE
FELLOWSHIP
OF THE RING

J. R. R. TOLKIEN

THE TWO
TOWERS

J. R. R. TOLKIEN

THE
RETURN OF
THE KING

J. R. R. TOLKIEN

"The English-speaking world is divided into those who have read *The Lord of the Rings* and those who are going to read them." SUNDAY TIMES

"Amongst the greatest works of imaginative fiction of the twentieth century." SUNDAY TELEGRAPH

"Masterpiece? Oh yes!" EVENING STANDARD

Des Plaines, 1955

McDonald's™ #1 open for business

HAMBURGER 15C
FRENCH FRIES 10C

(And no complaints about either being bad for your diet!)

Grace Kelly

Monaco

MOON OVER MONTE CARLO

This near bankrupt gambling principality was suddenly swelled by an invasion of wildly ill-assorted guests come to view the marriage of the screen-star daughter of an American bricklayer turned millionaire to Monaco's own Serene Highness, Prince Rainier III.

Somewhere behind the phantasmagoria of publicity, two human beings were approaching a solemn moment in St. Nicholas Cathedral. Rainier slipped the wedding ring onto Grace Kelly's finger, and the royal yacht bore the happy couple off.

For Grace Kelly Grimaldi and her Graustarkian Prince, it was only the beginning.

TIME Magazine, 30 April, 1956.

Grace Patricia Kelly married His Serene Highness Prince Rainier III of Monaco on April 19, 1956.

"The Wedding of the Year!

Grace Kelly's wedding dress was designed by Helen Rose, the costume designer for *High Society*. The dress was made from 98 yards of tulle, 25 yards of silk taffeta and 300 yards of lace. The veil was covered in a web of thousands of seed pearls with a motif of lovebirds appliquéd in lace."

FILMOGRAPHY

Fourteen Hours
High Noon
Mogambo
Rear Window
Green Fire
Dial M for Murder
The Country Girl*
The Bridges at Toko-Ri
To Catch a Thief
The Swan
High Society

*Won Best Actress,
1955 Academy Awards®.

Grace Kelly's movies are banned in Monaco, by order of Prince Rainier.

Rocky Marciano "THE BROCKTON BLOCKBUSTER"

1950's Career Stats:

(W)

(KO)

(KO)

(KO)

(W)

(KO)

(KO)

(KO)

(KO)

(W)

(KO)

(KO)

(KO)

(KO)

(KO)

(KO)

(KO)

(KO 13 –
wins world heavyweight title)

(KO 1 – retains title)

(KO 11 – retains title)

(W 15 – retains title)

(KO 8 – retains title)

(KO 9 – retains title)

(KO 9 – retains title)

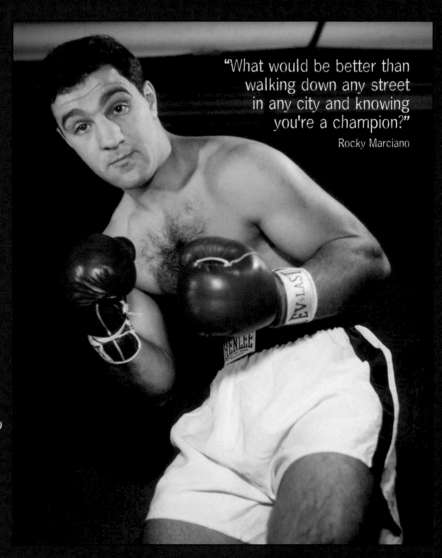

"What would be better than walking down any street in any city and knowing you're a champion?"

Rocky Marciano

"SWEET AS SUGAR"

Sugar Ray Robinson became the world welterweight champion in 1946 – a title which he held for five years and a reign that included a 91 fight winning-streak. He won the world middleweight title in 1951 which he held five times between 1951-1960.

Sugar Ray's record was 179 wins including 109 knockouts, 19 draws and six losses with two no contests in 206 professional bouts. In over 200 fights, Sugar Ray was never physically knocked out (though he did receive one technical KO).

"My business is hurting people."
Sugar Ray Robinson

1950's Career Stats

Jan 30, 1950 – George LaRover, New Haven

Feb 13, 1950 – Al Mobley, Miami

Feb 22, 1950 – Aaron Wade, Savannah

Feb 27, 1950 – Jean Walzack, St. Louis (W 10)

Mar 22, 1950 – George Costner, Philadelphia

Apr 21, 1950 – Cliff Beckett, Columbus

Apr 28, 1950 – Ray Barnes, Detroit (W 10)

Jun 5, 1950 – Robert Villemain, Philadelphia (W 15 – wins Pennsylvania middleweight title)

Aug 9, 1950 – Charley Fusari, Jersey City (W 15 – retains world welterweight title)

Aug 25, 1950 – Jose Basora, Scranton (KO 1 – retains Pennsylvania middleweight title)

Sep 4, 1950 – Billy Brown, New York (W 10)

Oct 16, 1950 – Joe Rindone, Boston (KO 6)

Oct 26, 1950 – Carl "Bobo" Olson, Philadelphia (KO 12 – retains Pennsylvania middleweight title)

Nov 8, 1950 – Bobby Dykes, Chicago (W 10)

Nov 27, 1950 – Jean Stock, Paris (KO 2)

Dec 9, 1950 – Luc Van Dam, Brussels (KO 4)

Dec 16, 1950 – Jean Walzack, Geneva (W 10)

Dec 22, 1950 – Robert Villemain, Paris (KO 9)

Dec 25, 1950 – Hans Stretz, Frankfurt (KO 5)

Feb 14, 1951 – Jake LaMotta, Chicago (KO 13 – wins world middleweight title and vacates world welterweight title)

Apr 5, 1951 – Holly Mims, Miami (W 10)

Apr 9, 1951 – Don Ellis, Oklahoma City (KO 1)

May 21, 1951 – Kid Marcel, Paris

May 26, 1951 – Jean Wanes, Zurich (W 10)

Jun 10, 1951 – Jan deBruin, Antwerp (KO 8)

Jun 16, 1951 – Jean Walzack, Luxembourg (KO 6)

Jun 24, 1951 – Gerhard Hecht, Berlin

Jul 1, 1951 – Cyrille Delannoit, Turin, Italy (KO 3)

Jul 10, 1951 – Randy Turpin, London (L 15 – loses world middleweight title)

Sep 12, 1951 – Randy Turpin, New York (KO 10 – regains world middleweight title)

Mar 13, 1952 – Carl "Bobo" Olson, San Francisco (W 15 – retains world middleweight title)

Apr 16, 1952 – Rocky Graziano, Chicago (KO 3 – retains world middleweight title)

Jun 25, 1952 – Joey Maxim, New York (KO 14 – bid at world light heavyweight title)

Dec 18, 1952 – Announces Retirement

Oct 20, 1954 – Announces Comeback

Nov 29, 1954 – Gene Burton, Hamilton, Ontario (Exh 6)

Jan 5, 1955 – Joe Rindone, Detroit (KO 6)

Jan 19, 1955 – Ralph "Tiger" Jones, Chicago (L 10)

Mar 29, 1955 – Johnny Lombardo, Cincinnati (W 10)

Apr 14, 1955 – Ted Olla, Milwaukee (KO 3)

May 4, 1955 – Garth Panter, Detroit (W 10)

Jul 22, 1955 – Rocky Castellani, San Francisco (W 10)

Dec 9, 1955 – Carl "Bobo" Olson, Chicago (KO 2 – regains world middleweight title)

May 18, 1956 – Carl "Bobo" Olson, Los Angeles (KO 4 – retains world middleweight title)

Nov 10, 1956 – Bob Provizzi, New Haven (W 10)

Jan 2, 1957 – Gene Fullmer, New York (L 15 – loses world middleweight title)

May 1, 1957 – Gene Fullmer, Chicago (KO 5 – regains world middleweight title)

Sep 10, 1957 – Otis Woodard, Philadelphia (Exh 2)

Sep 10, 1957 – Cosby Linson, Philadelphia (Exh 2)

Sep 23, 1957 – Carmen Basilio, New York (L 15 – loses world middleweight title)

Mar 25, 1958 – Carmen Basilio, Chicago (W 15 – regains world middleweight title)

Dec 14, 1959 – Bob Young, Boston (KO 2)

SLIM AT WILL!

Wash away excess fat – any part of the body.

Reduce arms, legs, hips – any part – in your bath, with Dr. Paul Bouchaud's Flesh-Reducing Soap. Get, and stay, smart and slim by this safe, easy home method, obtainable only from Madame B. Eugene, French hair and skin specialist. 1956

DRINK HABIT DESTROYED

Thousands of homes ruined by drink have been made happy again by Eucrasy. All desire for alcohol is destroyed. Guaranteed harmless, tasteless, can be given secretly or voluntarily. State which is wanted. 1956

OUTRAGEOUS ADVERTISING

HOW TO MAKE YOUR HUSBAND SAY, "YES!"

Tell him what an Alexander Smith Stay Modern carpet offers you for the price of a couple of bus fares a day.

FREE! Convincer Kit, practically guaranteed to make your husband say yes. Contains complete "we need new carpet" campaign, including booklet telling how to stretch your carpet dollar. 1955

TOO TIRED TO ENJOY LIFE?

Does the pace of modern living make you feel tired, nervy and depressed – spoiling both work and leisure? What to do?

Doctors often prescribe yeast with its vitality vitamins. Now, thanks to modern medicine, there is an improvement. It's called Chloro-Yeast, and in addition to active yeast, it contains valuable analgesics and tonics – plus special chlorophyll to keep body and breath free of odor. Chloro-Yeast tones up tired, tense, worried people in double-quick time, yet tranquillizes as it does so. Very likely this is just what your system needs. Certainly it's worth trying a bottle of these safe, effective tablets. Available at good pharmacies and stores everywhere. Carefully note the name – CHLORO-YEAST. 1957

NO MORE BALD HEADS!

...when our vacuum cap is used a few minutes daily.

The vacuum cap is an appliance that draws the blood to the hair roots and starts a new healthy crop of hair. It stops dandruff, stops the hair from falling out. No drugs used. Sent on free trial. Illustrated folder and testimonials sent without obligation. Plain covers. Free catalogues also sent on slimming foam wonder bath crystals and amazing denture plastic Fit-Rite. On application dentures fit anew during life of denture. Develop a beautiful figure by increasing the bust with Charm Bust gentle pulsavator. 1956

CLAIMS

ELIMINATE THAT DOUBLE CHIN

A new way for more beauty. 15 minutes daily while reading or working will eliminate a double chin, sagging throat line, hanging cheeks and wrinkled neck. Made of highly elastic smooth rubber, supported by 4 adjustable headbands; fits every chin and is very simple to slip on. 1959

"If you're a man between the ages of 18 and 80, Playboy is meant for you. If you like your entertainment served up with humor, sophistication and spice, Playboy will become a very special favorite."

Extract from the first issue

The first issue was published in December 1953. It cost 50 cents, and sold 54,175 copies. It was undated because Hugh Hefner didn't know if there would be a second issue... he also didn't put his name on it in case it was a failure.

"He buys it
for the
articles…"

In 1950 there were more than 40 million telephones in use in the US alone. 75% of telephone lines in the US however were still party lines.

On February 18, 1950 the first long-distance telephone service in the US commenced between New York and New Jersey, eliminating the need for operator assisted calls.

The first telephone pager device was used by the Jewish Hospital in New York in 1950. These were not consumer units and the device would not win FCC approval until 1958.

In 1950, the first coin telephone mobile train service was established on the Pennsylvania Railroad between New York and Washington.

In 1952, telephones with illuminated dials were introduced.

A special "test" number, 555-5555, was reserved to allow testing by telephone companies. The number was adopted by television shows and movies but no number with the prefix "555" will ever reach a real number.

In 1954 Western Electric began production of color telephones in eight shades.

On March 4, 1955, the first radio facsimile transmission was sent across the US.

"Transmission of documents via telephone wires is possible in principle, but the apparatus required is so expensive that it will never become a practical proposition." Dennis Gabor

THE PRINCESS® TELEPHONE
"It's Little, it's Lovely, and it Lights!"

The **50 millionth** telephone was installed on November 18, 1956 on the desk of President Eisenhower. **59 million** telephones would be in operation in the US by the end of 1956.

In September 1959, Bell launched the "Princess"® telephone which had a dial that illuminated when the handset was lifted. Designed to appeal to women it allowed people to "match" the décor of different rooms and the first model was available in white, beige, pink, blue or turquoise.

The Platters   Little Anthony and the Imperials   The Crests   The Coasters

The Four Tops

The Penguins

The Solitaires

Frankie Lymon and the
The Teenagers

The Clovers   The Crows   The Chords   The Blue Caps

The Dominoes The Fiestas The Ravens The Orioles

The Drifters

The Harptones

The Diamonds The Del-Vikings The Fleetwoods The Cadillacs

DR. SEUSS

Theodor Seuss Geisel

Horton Hears a Who!
August 1954

The Cat in the Hat
March 1957

How the Grinch Stole Christmas!
October 1957

**The Cat in the Hat
Comes Back**
September 1958

"Be who you are and say what
you feel, because those who mind
don't matter and those who
matter don't mind."
                    Dr. Seuss

ELOISE

by Kay Thompson,
Illustrated by Hilary Knight

Eloise: a book for precocious grown ups
November 1955

Eloise in Paris
November 1957

Eloise at Christmastime
September 1958

Eloise in Moscow
October 1959

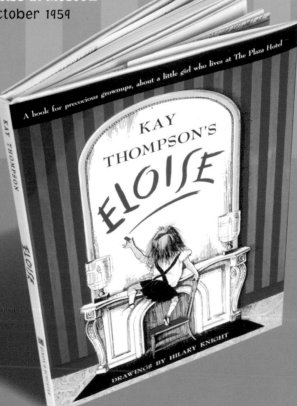

"The Eloise boom is not likely to make little girls more remarkably fiendish than they already are. That isn't possible."

Kay Thompson quoted in Life magazine, December 9, 1957

THIS IS CINERAMA

"Plunges you into a startling new world."

Outboard motor boats sail through the air with the greatest of ease in *This is Cinerama*.

This is Cinerama premiered in New York City on September 30, 1952, and was the highest grossing movie of that year. The Cinerama format was introduced to the UK in 1954.

The unique Cinerama image is formed by shooting on three separate 35mm films and sound is carried on a fourth 35mm magnetic film with 7 soundtracks. The individual frames were six perforations high instead of the usual four and the frame rate was increased from 24 to 26 frames per second to reduce the apparent flicker on the giant 146 degree screen. Cinerama's three frames formed an image of approximately six times the definition of conventional 35mm film and combined with sharp wide angle lenses with their extended depth of field, made for an unparalleled viewing experience.

"Puts you in the picture!"

Cinerama movies were projected onto a 146 degree curved screen 32 feet high and 78 feet wide, using three projectors and accompanied by seven tracks of stereo sound.

The total US box office gross for Cinerama shows from 1952 to 1959 was $93 million.

Cinerama was so popular that two other rival 3-panel processes were developed: Cinemiracle, and a Soviet version called Kinopanorama. Hollywood also developed wide screen formats including CinemaScope, Technirama, Todd AO, VistaVision, Wonderama, and Panavision.

"so exciting you'll grab your leg!"

MOVIES

This Is Cinerama, Cinerama Holiday, Seven Wonders of the World, Search For Paradise, South Seas Adventure, Windjammer, The Wonderful World of the Brothers Grimm, The Best of Cinerama, How the West was Won

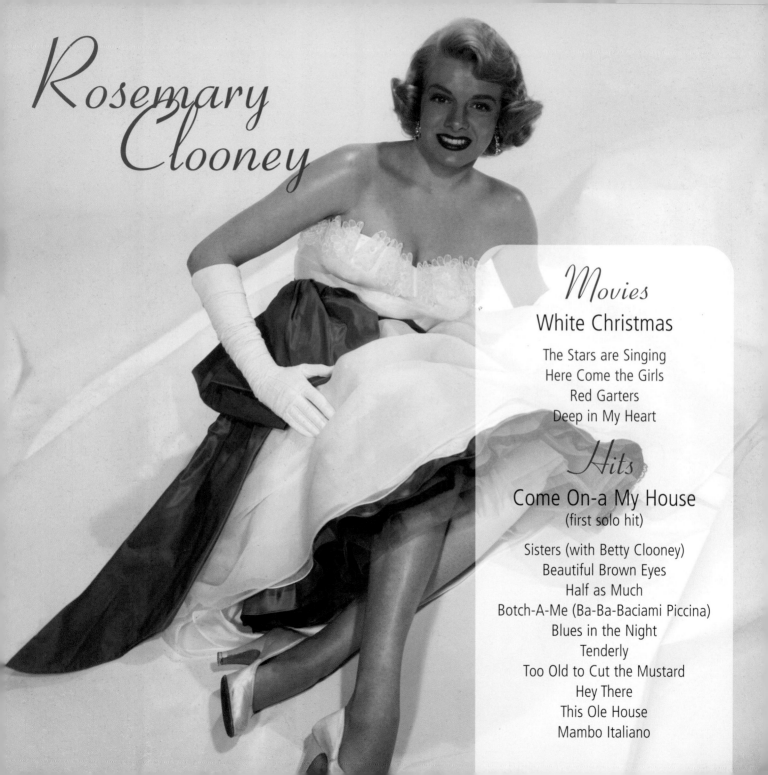

Rosemary Clooney

Movies
White Christmas

The Stars are Singing
Here Come the Girls
Red Garters
Deep in My Heart

Hits

Come On-a My House
(first solo hit)

Sisters (with Betty Clooney)
Beautiful Brown Eyes
Half as Much
Botch-A-Me (Ba-Ba-Baciami Piccina)
Blues in the Night
Tenderly
Too Old to Cut the Mustard
Hey There
This Ole House
Mambo Italiano

Patti Page
"the singing rage"

Hits
Tennessee Waltz

All My Love (Bolero)
Detour
Mister and Mississippi
Mockn' bird Hill
Come What May
I Went to Your Wedding
The Doggie In the Window
Changing Partners
Steam Heat
Cross Over the Bridge
Allegheny Moon
Old Cape Cod

THE
ED SULLIVAN SHOW
"THE GREAT STONE FACE"

Toast of the Town
1948 – 1955

The Ed Sullivan Show
1955 – 1971

THE FAMOUS
"ELVIS" APPEARANCE

Elvis Presley was paid an
incredible **$50,000** to appear.
The show aired on September 9, 1956.

"I want to say to Elvis Presley
and the country that this is a real,
decent fine boy, and we never
had a pleasanter experience on our
show with a big name than
we've had with you."

*Ed Sullivan to Elvis in front of the studio
audience after Elvis' third appearance on
The Ed Sullivan Show, January 6, 1957.*

The Tonight Show
1954 – 1957

Host: **Steve Allen**
Announcer: **Gene Rayburn**

"Hi-Ho Steverino!"

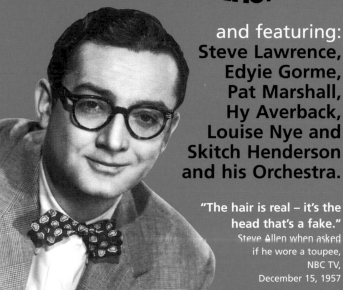

and featuring:
**Steve Lawrence,
Edyie Gorme,
Pat Marshall,
Hy Averback,
Louise Nye and
Skitch Henderson
and his Orchestra.**

"The hair is real – it's the
head that's a fake."
Steve Allen when asked
if he wore a toupee,
NBC TV,
December 15, 1957

The Jack Paar
Tonight Show
1957 – 1962

"Paar's mind is one part genius and two parts
chocolate fudge."
Anonymous television critic

Announcer: **Hugh Downs**
Bandleader: **Jose Melis**

and featuring: **Dody Goodman,
Elsa Maxwell,
Jonathan Winters,
Peggy Cass,
Cliff Arquette.**

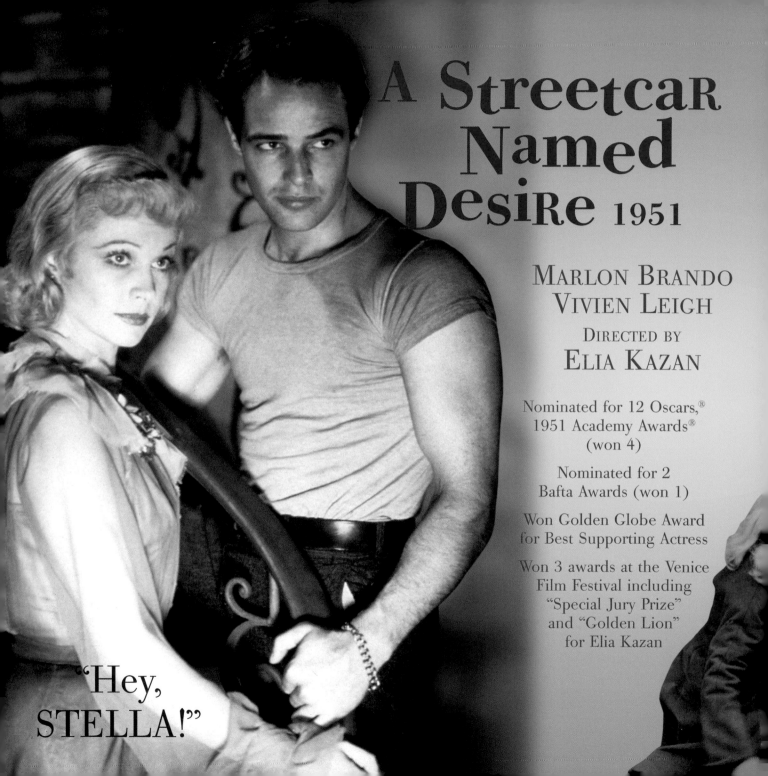

A Streetcar Named Desire 1951

MARLON BRANDO
VIVIEN LEIGH

DIRECTED BY
ELIA KAZAN

Nominated for 12 Oscars,®
1951 Academy Awards®
(won 4)

Nominated for 2
Bafta Awards (won 1)

Won Golden Globe Award
for Best Supporting Actress

Won 3 awards at the Venice
Film Festival including
"Special Jury Prize"
and "Golden Lion"
for Elia Kazan

"Hey,
STELLA!"

On the Waterfront 1954

Nominated for 12 Oscars,®
1955 Academy Awards®
(won 8)

Nominated for 3 Bafta Awards
(won 1)

Won 4 Golden Globe Awards

Won 3 awards at the Venice Film Festival

Won Director's Guild of America Award
for "Outstanding Directional
Achievement in Motion Pictures"

Won Writers Guild of America award for
"Best Written American Drama"

MARLON BRANDO
EVA MARIE SAINT
DIRECTED BY ELIA KAZAN

"You don't understand.
I coulda' had class. I coulda'
been a contender. I coulda' been
someone, Charley, instead of
a bum, which is what I am.
Let's face it. I'm a bum."

Inaugural flight

The first jet-powered commercial flight was on May 2, 1952, from London to Johannesburg, by B.O.A.C. using a De Havilland Comet.

The flight departed from London's Heathrow airport, stopping at Rome, Cairo, Khartoum, Entebbe and Livingston, before touching down in Johannesburg. Total flight time was 23 hours, 40 minutes.

The first trans-Atlantic flight was also made by B.O.A.C. on October 4, 1958. The flight took 8 hours and 53 minutes.

WE'RE FLYING YEARS AHEAD!

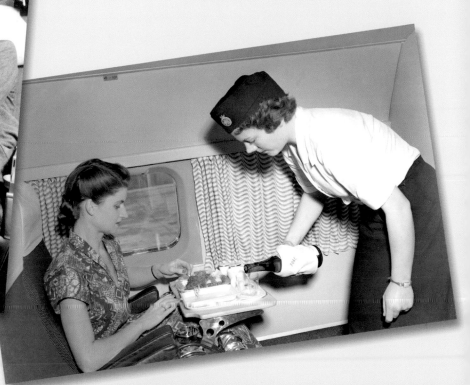

The New Comet 4

Fitted out to carry

36 passengers

in comfort!

Passengers relaxing on the sleeper seats in the new Comet 4.

Popular with teenagers in the mid-50s, the poodle or circle skirt is a wide swing skirt with a poodle appliquéd or transferred onto the fabric.

Poodles were not the only items used to adorn these skirts — flowers, records, cars and other animals were also popular.

Known as "Bobby Soxers," the look was completed with a Peter Pan shirt, a cardigan and a neck-scarf which also doubled as a pony tail tie. Essential footwear was saddle shoes — stiff leather shoes with a brown or black "saddle" over the mid-part of the shoe — penny loafers, colored sneakers, sandals or ballet slippers.

Hair was either pulled back in a pony tail or held back with a headband.

Bobby Soxers

The male equivalents of "Bobby Soxers" were "Ivy League" or "preppy." Wardrobe essentials included cardigan sweaters, which were also used for the "letter sweater" so popular among athletes.

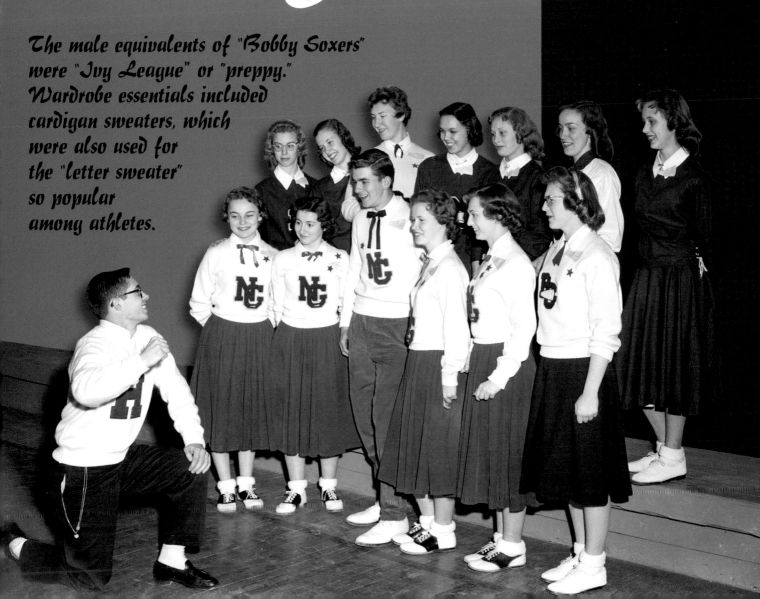

"Television won't last. It's a flash in the pan."

Mary Somerville, pioneer of radio educational broadcasts

TELEVISION IN REVIEW: NBC Color

Tournament of Roses Parade is Sent Over 22-City Network

The Tournament of Roses parade, received locally from 12:15 to 1:45 P.M., did emphasize several problems for the home viewer. In the broad daylight and sunshine, it was necessary to draw the shades and cut out all glare if the colors on the TV screen were not to be washed out. This frankly, was a nuisance.

Another difficulty related to the size of the picture. The disadvantage of a small color image - roughly 12 1/2 inches - was much more noticeable with the parade than with earlier studio programs. And, since it is necessary to sit much farther away than from a black and white set, one wonders how big a color tube will be practical. Finding a happy compromise between picture size and viewing distance could be tricky for the engineer and the viewer, particularly if the latter must start rearranging furniture again.

NEW YORK TIMES. Monday January 4, 1954

"The average American family hasn't time for television."

The New York Times

Commercial Television Commences

The BBC started regular television transmission in the UK in 1936 but ceased between 1939 and 1946 due to WWII. The first regularly scheduled television broadcasts in the US began in 1939.

1950 – Mexico
1951 - The Netherlands
1952 – Italy, Germany
1953 – Japan, Switzerland, Belgium
1954 – Poland, Finland, Monaco, Czechoslovakia, Hungary

1955 – Luxembourg, Denmark, Austria
1956 – Yugoslavia, Australia, Sweden
1957 – Portugal
1958 – China
1959 – Spain, India

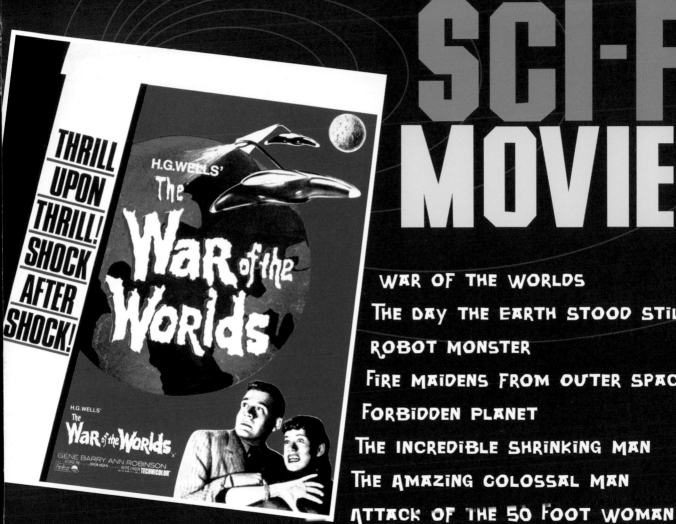

"Not since the **beginning** of **time** has the world beheld **terror** like this!"

SCI-FI MOVIES

WAR OF THE WORLDS

THE DAY THE EARTH STOOD STILL

ROBOT MONSTER

FIRE MAIDENS FROM OUTER SPACE

FORBIDDEN PLANET

THE INCREDIBLE SHRINKING MAN

THE AMAZING COLOSSAL MAN

ATTACK OF THE 50 FOOT WOMAN

THE COLOSSUS OF NEW YORK

THE MOST PERFECTLY PLANNED TOWN IN AMERICA!

Levittown

LEVITTOWN NASSAU COUNTY, LONG ISLAND, NEW YORK
(completed 1951)

LEVITTOWN PENNSYLVANIA
(completed 1952)

The Levittowner: Price $9,990. **The Country Clubber:** Price $16,990. **The Budgeter:** Rent $65 a month.

Pat Boone

"I once shook hands with Pat Boone and my whole right side sobered up."

Dean Martin

Pat Boone's trademark style was a pair of "white bucks" — a patent leather shoe style popular for a time in the 50s.

"Love Letters In the Sand" was his biggest selling hit, selling 3 million records, and topping the US charts for 5 weeks.

Bing Crosby

"He would sing at the drop of a hat. He would sing all the time. He'd sing when he was riding a bicycle, he'd sing when he was walking down the street, he'd sing on a train — he had a singing habit."

Rosemary Clooney

Bing Crosby made more studio recordings than any other singer in history.

"White Christmas" is the only single to make American pop charts 20 times.

The first "made for tv" movie was "High Tor" in 1956 starring Bing Crosby and co-starring Julie Andrews.

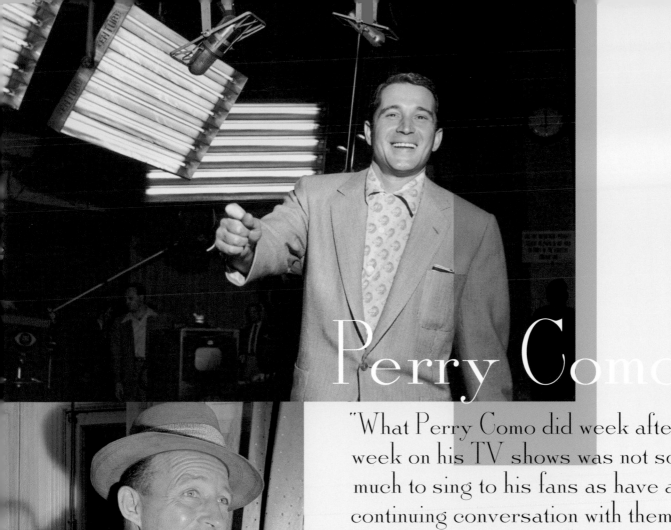

Perry Como

"What Perry Como did week after week on his TV shows was not so much to sing to his fans as have a continuing conversation with them, a conversation in song." Washington Post

Perry Como was the first male solo artist to win a Grammy Award. The "Perry Como Show" ran on NBC from 1948 to 1950, on CBS from 1950 to 1955 and again on NBC from 1955 to 1963, becoming the third-longest running TV show ever, behind "Gunsmoke" and "Lassie."

ROBBY THE ROBOT!

STAR OF: Forbidden Planet, The Invisible Boy, The Twilight Zone,
Lost In Space, Ark II, Star Wars, Mork & Mindy, Gremlins, Cherry 2000

M·G·M PRESENTS FORBIDDEN PLANET

IN CINEMASCOPE AND COLOR

STARRING

WALTER ANNE LESLIE
PIDGEON · FRANCIS · NIELSEN

With WARREN STEVENS And Introducing ROBBY, THE ROBOT

Screen Play by CYRIL HUME · Based on a Story by IRVING BLOCK and ALLEN ADLER · Photographed in EASTMAN COLOR

Directed by FRED McLEOD WILCOX

Produced by NICHOLAS NAYFACK

AN M·G·M PICTURE

AMAZING

The Honeymooners
1955-1956

"The Jackie Gleason Show" went to air on September 20, 1952.

"The Honeymooners" was part of "The Jackie Gleason Show" but from October 1, 1955 to September 22, 1956, 39 episodes aired as a separate show.

STARRING
Jackie "I got a big mouth" Gleason
as Ralph Kramden
Art Carney as Ed Norton
Pert Kelton as Alice Kramden (1951-1952)
Audrey Meadows as Alice Kramden
(1952-1961)
Joyce Randolph as Trixie Norton

FATHER KNOWS BEST
1954-1963

"Father Knows Best" started out as a radio show in 1949 before debuting on October 3, 1954 on CBS.

STARRING
Robert Young as James "Jim" Anderson
Jane Wyatt as Margaret Anderson
Elinor Donahue as Betty "Princess" Anderson
Billy Gray as James "Bud" Anderson Jr.
Lauren Chapin as Kathy "Kitten" Anderson

families!

The Adventures of *Ozzie and Harriet*

1953-1956

Originally a radio series "The Adventures of Ozzie & Harriet" aired from October 3, 1953 to September 3, 1956.

STARRING

Ozzie Nelson as Ozzie Nelson
Harriet Hillard Nelson as Harriet Nelson
David Nelson as David Nelson
Ricky Nelson as Ricky Nelson

Leave it to Beaver

1957-1963

Originally called "Wally and Beaver," "Leave it to Beaver" first aired on October 4, 1957.

STARRING

Jerry Mathers as Theodore "Beaver" Cleaver
Barbara Billingsley as June Cleaver
Hugh Beaumont as Ward Cleaver
Tony Dow as Wallace "Wally" Cleaver

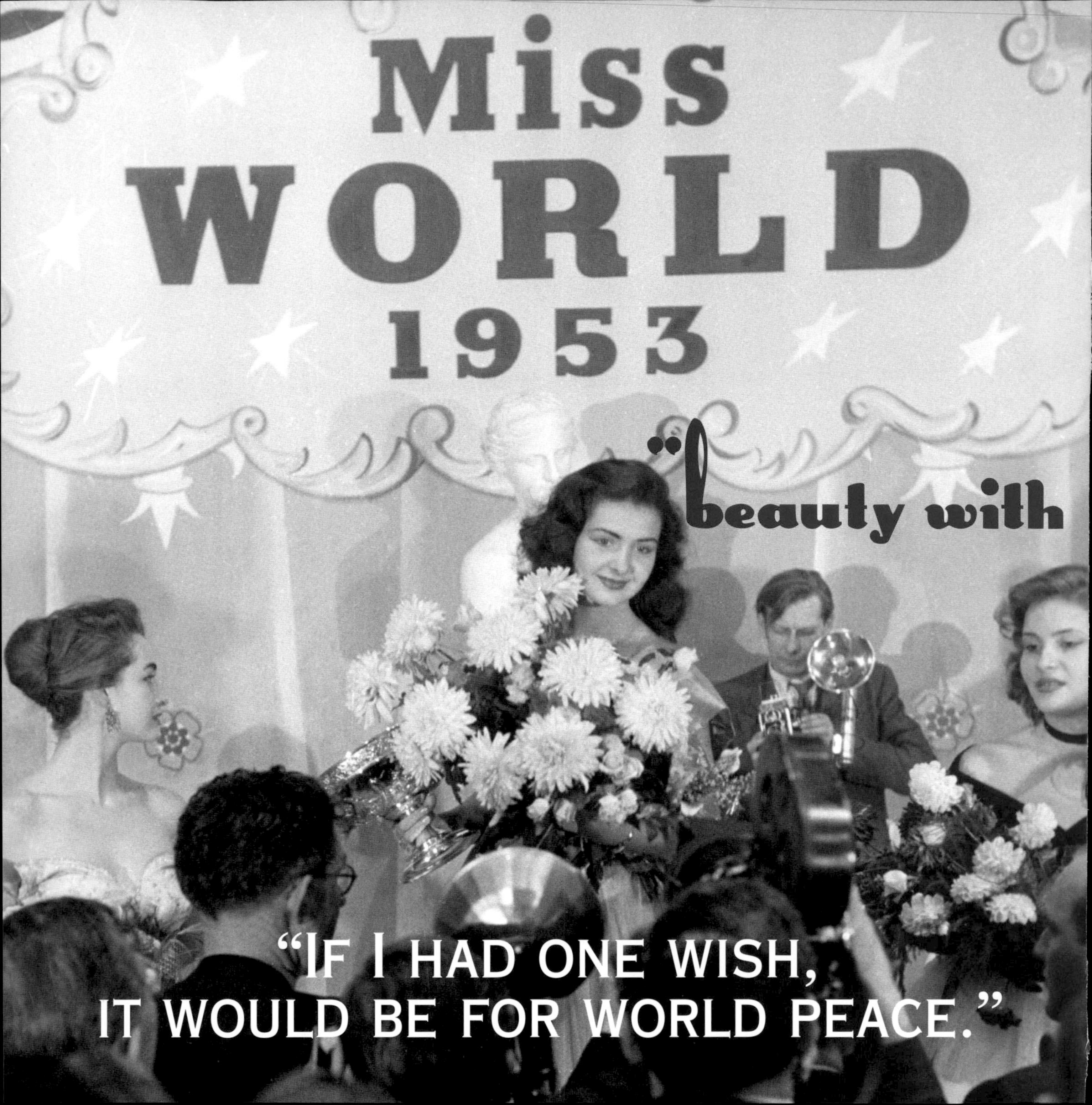

“beauty with

“IF I HAD ONE WISH,
IT WOULD BE FOR WORLD PEACE.”

The pageant was originally called the
"Festival Bikini Contest"
but was dubbed "Miss World" by
the local media, and creator
Eric Morley trademarked the name.

The competition was first
televised on the BBC in 1959.

a purpose.

The first Miss World won a cheque for
GBP £1,000 and a pearl necklace.

WINNERS in the 50s

1951	Miss Sweden, Kerstin "Kiki" Haakonson
1952	Miss Sweden, May Louise Flodin
1953	Miss France, Denise Perrier
1954	Miss Egypt, Antigone Constanda
1955	Miss Venezuela, Carmen Susana Duijm Zubillaga
1956	Miss Germany, Petra Susanna Schürmann
1957	Miss Finland, Marita Lindahl
1958	Miss South Africa, Penelope Anne Coelen
1959	Miss The Netherlands, Corinne Rottschafer

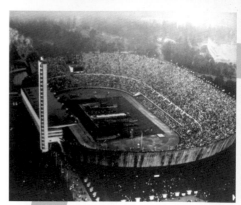

HELSINKI

July 19 - August 3

1952

Czechoslovakia's Emil Zatopek produced one of the greatest performances in distance running history.

He won the 5,000m, successfully defended his 10,000m title and then took his third gold medal in his first-ever marathon race to complete a triple which remains unique in Olympic history.

MELBOURNE

November 22 - December 8

1956

DID YOU KNOW...

The Melbourne Games were the first Olympics to be held in the Southern Hemisphere. Because of strict Australian quarantine rules, the equestrian events were held in Stockholm in June.

Menu

Drinks

Milk · Orange Juice · Tea · Coffee · Hot Chocolate · Coca-Cola · Soda Water · Dr. Pepper
Root Beer · Malted Milk · Milkshakes – Vanilla, Strawberry, Chocolate · Ice Cream Sodas

Food

Doughnuts · Toast – rye or white · Eggs – any style · Hash · Western Omelette · Waffles
Sausage · Pancakes · Ham sandwich · Tuna salad sandwich · Tuna fish sandwich
Grilled cheese sandwich · Cheese and bacon sandwich · Bacon, lettuce and tomato sandwich
Hamburger (with or without onions) · Hot dog · Hot dog and sauerkraut · Franks and beans
Baked beans · Hungarian Goulash · Beef Stew · Pea Soup · Tomato Soup · French fries
Chilli con carne · Liver and onions · Cracker biscuits and cheese · Spaghetti · Bread and
butter · Spare Ribs · Corned beef and
cabbage · Ground beef on toast · Sausages
and mashed potato · Baked potato

Dessert

Jello · Rice pudding · Ice cream
Vanilla Pudding · Custard Pie
Apple Pie with cheese · Blueberry Pie
Banana Split · Chocolate pudding
Tapioca Pudding · Apple Pie

Diner Slang

Soup jockey (waitress)
Ladybug (fountain man)
Bubble Dancer (dishwasher)
Angel (sandwich man)
Gallery (booth)
Eighty-six ("Do not sell to that customer" or "The kitchen is out of the item ordered.")
Let it walk, On wheels (an order to go)
In the alley (served as a side dish)
No cow (without milk)

Gravel train (sugar bowl) · Canned cow (evaporated milk) · Hold the hail (no ice)
Dog soup (glass of water) · Pigs in a blanket (a ham or sausage sandwich)
Radio Sandwich (tuna fish sandwich) · One from the Alps (Swiss cheese sandwich)
GAC, Jack (grilled American cheese sandwich) · Burn one (put a hamburger on the grill)
Million on a platter (a plate of baked beans) · Frog sticks (French fries)
Two cows, make them cry (two hamburgers with onions)
Whiskey Down (rye toast)

DOLL'S HOSPITAL
—IN PATIENTS—
SURGERY HOURS
9 A.M. to 6

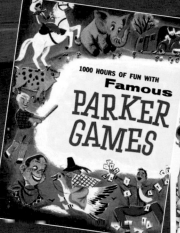

1000 HOURS OF FUN WITH
Famous
PARKER GAMES

SPECIAL *Joy* OFFER!
Get several for Gifts!

Walking
Doll only 50¢

She actually walks—her head moves, too!

SEND NOW
BEFORE JOY'S SPECIAL OFFER ENDS!

THRIFTY SANTAS SHOP AT... **Gambles**

AS LOW AS 50¢ DOWN

Menswear

"It fits snug as your skin, moves as you move, gives you positive masculine support... it's your assurance that you're getting the famous Coopers product — and one of the many reason why Jockey gives you a real lift."

Jockey Underwear. 1950

give the gift that lasts...

FRUIT OF THE LOOM UNDERWEAR

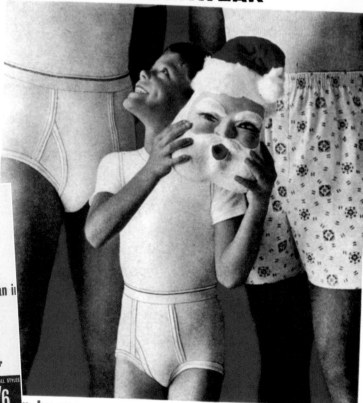

n by more men and boys than any other brand

Y'S MEN WEAR Y-FRONT!

look good..feel good..be twice the man i

Y-FRONT Coopers
REGD. & PATENTED

the first and finest men's support underwear

The modern conception of underwear comfort... trim, snug, absorbent, hygienic... sized to fit YOU. No buttons, no tapes, easy to launder, and with the unique Y-Front support construction. SHORTS AND SINGLETS (as on left) IN PANEL RIB OR COTTON MESH.

Alternative styles in Panel Rib Cotton

Short sleeved Vests and Midways

ALL SIZES - ALL STYLES
6'6
PER GARMENT

Y-FRONT IS MADE ONLY BY Lyle and Scott OF SCOTTISH KNITWEAR FAM

"Fun for all...
and all for fun...
in Weldon's gay, colorful, happily
comfortable "Islander" Pajamas...just
the ticket for a pleasant evening of
playing the Pajama Game together."
Weldon Pajamas, 1957

"Make like a medicine
man in Voodoo shorts.
Munsingwear gives you a chance to
show her... you can be just as wild and
original with your shorts as she is with
her hats. Loud, laughing colors that seem to
chant a reckless rhythm." Munsingwear, 1951

"Wear a Hat —
It's as Healthy as
It's Handsome!"
Hat Corporation of America — Makers of
Fine Hats for Men and Women, 1952

"The story you have just seen is true.
Only the names have been changed to protect the innocent." Dragnet

> "Peter Gunn – suave, sophisticated, hep to the jive, groovin' to the jazzbo-beat private eye."

Peter Gunn
1958 – 1960

STARRING
CRAIG STEVENS as PETER GUNN
LOLA ALBRIGHT as EDIE HART
HOPE EMERSON as MOTHER
HERSCHEL BERNARDI as
LIEUTENANT JACOBY
Music by HENRY MANCINI

Dragnet
1952 – 1959

STARRING
JACK WEBB as JOE FRIDAY
BEN ALEXANDER as FRANK SMITH
HERBERT ELLIS as
OFFICER FRANK SMITH (1952)
GEORGE FENNEMAN as
ANNOUNCER (1952 – 1959)
BARNEY PHILLIPS as
ED JACOBS (1952)
BARTON YARBOROUGH as
BEN ROMERO (1951)

77 Sunset Strip
1958 – 1964

STARRING
EFREM ZIMBALIST JNR. as
STUART BAILEY
ROGER SMITH as JEFF SPENCER
EDD BYRNES as GERALD LLOYD
"KOOKIE" KOOKSON III
LOUIS QUINN as ROSCOE
JACQUELINE BEER as SUZANNE FABRAY
BYRON KEITH as LT. GILMORE
ROBERT LOGAN as J.R.HALE
RICHARD LONG as REX RANDOLPH
JOAN STALEY as HANNAH

> "That chick's the ginchiest."
>
> (I do believe that woman is attractive). *"Kookie"*

Perry Mason
1957 – 1966

STARRING
RAYMOND BURR as PERRY MASON
BARBARA HALE as DELLA STREET
WILLIAM HOPPER as PAUL DRAKE
WILLIAM TALMAN as
D.A. HAMILTON BURGER
RAY COLLINS as LIEUTENANT
ARTHUR TRAGG
CONNIE CEZAN as GERTIE LADE

> "Special Agent Eliot Ness and his elite team of incorruptible agents battle organized crime in 1930s Chicago."

The Untouchables
1959 – 1963

STARRING
ROBERT STACK as ELIOT NESS
FRANK WILCOX as DISTRICT
ATTORNEY BEECHER ASBURY
WALTER WINCHELL as NARRATOR
ABEL FERNANDEZ as
AGENT WILLIAM YOUNGFELLOW
NICHOLAS GEORGIADE as
AGENT ENRICO ROSSI
BRUCE GORDON as FRANK NITTI
STEVE LONDON as
AGENT JACK ROSSMAN
JERRY PARIS as AGENT MARTIN
FLAHERTY (1959-1960)

OTHER SHOWS

MARTIN KANE, PRIVATE EYE (1949-1954)
MAN AGAINST CRIME (1949-1956)
THE AMAZING MR. MALONE (1951-1952)
ELLERY QUEEN (1950-1952)
BIG TOWN (1950-1956)
NAKED CITY (1957-1963)
BOURBON STREET BEAT (1959-1960)
HAWAIIAN EYE (1959-1963)

NBA

Prior to the 1949-1950 season the National Basketball League (founded in 1937) and the Basketball Association of America (formed in 1946) merged to form the National Basketball Association.

The 24-second shot clock was adopted prior to the 1954-55 season. Syracuse owner, Danny Biasone, came up with the idea which along with a limit on the number of fouls a team could commit in a quarter, many believe saved the game.

The NBA's first African-American players entered the competition in 1950. Chuck Cooper was the first African-American to be drafted by an NBA team, Nat Clifton was the first to sign an NBA contract, and on October 31, 1950, Earl Lloyd, playing for the Washington Capitols, became the first African-American to play in an NBA game – one day before Clifton and Cooper.

THE SYRACUSE NATIONALS

NBA Originals:

THE BOSTON CELTICS

Boston Celtics
New York Knickerbockers
Philadelphia Warriors
Washington Capitols
Minneapolis Lakers
Fort Wayne Zollner Pistons
Rochester Royals
Syracuse Nationals
Tri-Cities Blackhawks
Indianapolis Olympians
Milwaukee Hawks
Chicago Stags
St. Louis Bombers
Baltimore Bullets
Anderson Duffey Packers
Sheboygan Redskins
Waterloo Hawks
Denver Nuggets

NBA Champions

1949 - 50	Minneapolis Lakers def. Syracuse Nationals 4-2
1950 - 51	Rochester Royals def. New York Knicks 4-3
1951 - 52	Minneapolis Lakers def. New York Knicks 4-3
1952 - 53	Minneapolis Lakers def. New York Knicks 4-1
1953 - 54	Minneapolis Lakers def. Syracuse Nationals 4-3
1954 - 55	Syracuse Nationals def. Fort Wayne Pistons 4-3
1955 - 56	Philadelphia Warriors def. Fort Wayne Pistons 4-1
1956 - 57	Boston Celtics def. St. Louis Hawks 4-3
1957 - 58	St. Louis Hawks def. Boston Celtics 4-2
1958 - 59	Boston Celtics def. Minneapolis Lakers 4-0
1959 - 60	Boston Celtics def. St. Louis Hawks 4-3

THE MINNEAPOLIS LAKERS

GEORGE MIKAN (99)

One of the tallest players in the game at 6' 10", Mikan was so hard to defend and score against that the NBA changed the rules of play to reduce his impact on the game. A key member of the Minneapolis Lakers, his tough style saw him complete a game with a broken leg, just one of 10 broken bones during his career.

BOB COUSY (14)

Nicknamed the "The Cooz" and "The Houdini of the Hardwood," Bob Cousy was a key member of the Boston Celtics known for his "razzle-dazzle" style. Won "Most Valuable Player" award 1956-57.

BOB PETTIT (9)

Bob Pettit had an 11-year career with the Milwaukee and St. Louis Hawks and was the first player to top 20,000 points. Won "Most Valuable Player" award twice in the 1950s for the 1955-56 and 1958-59 seasons.

BILL RUSSELL

Bill Russell joined the Boston Celtics in December 1956 having just won a gold medal at the Melbourne Olympic Games. The Celtics won 11 championships in his 13 seasons with the team. Won "Most Valuable Player" award 1957-58.

THERE IS NOTHING YOU CAN NAME

1958, starring
Mitzi Gaynor
and
Rossano Brazzi

Directed by
Joshua Logan

WRITTEN BY

OSCAR HAMMERSTEIN II

MUSIC BY

RICHARD RODGERS

Based on *Tales of the South Pacific* by
James A. Michener, winner of the
Pulitzer Prize in 1946. The stage musical
won the Pulitzer Prize in 1950 – the only
instance in Pulitzer history where a
single work has won the Pulitzer Prize
in two guises.

MUSICAL
**STARRING MARY MARTIN
AND EZIO PINZA**

Majestic Theatre, Broadway,
New York, 1949-1954
(and simultaneously undertook
a US tour of 118 cities)

Theatre Royal, Drury Lane, London, 1951

DID YOU KNOW...

Sean Connery's first acting part was in the chorus in the London stage production of *South Pacific*. A little known actor, Larry Hagman, also appeared in the chorus of the London production, due in part to his mother, Mary Martin, being the leading star of the stage production.

"I'M GONNA' WASH THAT MAN RIGHT OUT OF MY HAIR."

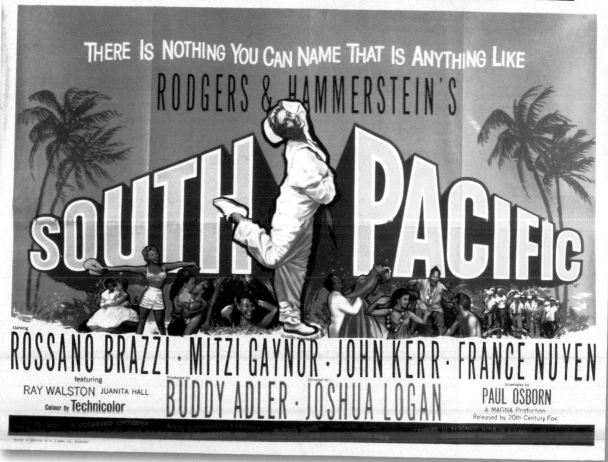

FIDELITY

Model 657. Stereophonic high-fidelity console phonograph, complete with 2 remote speakers. 20 watts, dual-channel amplifier. Automatic 4-speed record changer, with diamond stylus. Mahogany, $299.95 ... blond mahogany or walnut cabinets priced slightly higher.

Sit anywhere in the room

COLUMBIA STEREOPHONIC PHONOGRAPHS PUT YOU IN THE CENTER OF SOUND

Here is the ultimate in listening—a new Columbia stereophonic phonograph. Turn it on and you're suddenly, dramatically in the Center of Sound—the place where music takes on a third dimension. Turn the remarkable Balanced Listening Control and you shift the Center of Sound wherever you want it. This Columbia engineering exclusive, available on many models, makes it possible for you to enjoy stereophonic sound in perfect proportion —not just in one spot, but *anywhere in the room!* Superb styling and cabinetry make every Columbia Stereo-Fidelity phonograph a truly matchless instrument for your home. Prices begin at only $124.90.

STEREO-FIDELITY PHONOGRAPHS BY COLUMBIA ▣

A division of Columbia Broadcasting Systems, Inc. ® "Columbia" ℗ Marcas Reg. Prices are suggested list, slightly higher west of the Rockies.

"...new Columbia stereophonic phonograph. Turn it on and you're suddenly, dramatically in the Center of Sound   the place where music takes on a third dimension."

Advertisement for Columbia Stereophonic Phonographs, 1958

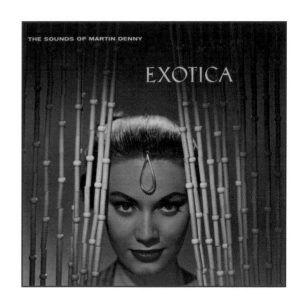

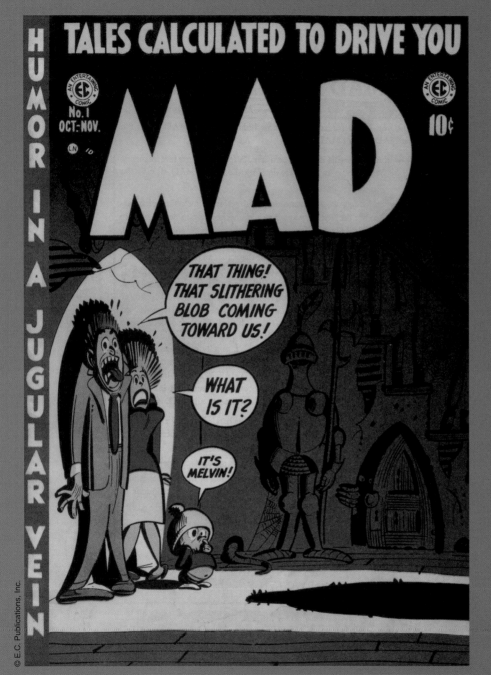

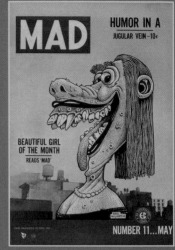

"MAD" MAGAZINE - ISSUE ONE, OCTOBER 1952

"BEETLE BAILEY"

by Mort Walker debuted as a college cutup in 1950 in 50 newspapers. The feature was quickly bought and syndicated by King Features and was the last strip personally approved by William Randolph Hearst.

Brylcreem, Brylcreem, Brylcreem,

Brylcreem, a little dab'll do ya!

Brylcreem, you'll look so debonair!

Brylcreem, the gals'll all pursue ya!

They'll love to get their fingers in your hair!

Brylcreem, a little dab'll do ya!

For watch out, the gals'll all pursue ya!

Use Ajax, the foaming and pans, just like a whiz, Use You'll stop paying the cleaning with Ajax, So use Ajax,

Floats the dirt right down the drain,

See the USA, in your Chevrolet,

America is asking you to call,

Drive your Chevrolet, through the USA,

America's the greatest land of all,

On a highway, or a road, along the levy,

Performance is sweeter, nothing can beat her,

Life is completer in a Chevy,

So make a date today, to see the USA,

And see it in your Chevrolet.

cleanser, Clean pots Ajax, the foaming cleanser, elbow tax, When you start the foaming cleanser, Soooo use Ajax.

I love Bosco, it's rich and chocolatey, Chocolate flavored Bosco is mighty good for me!, Mama puts it in my milk for extra energy, Bosco gives me iron, and sunshine Vitamin C! Oh I love Bosco, that's the drink for me.

It walks down stairs, alone and in pairs, and makes a slinking sound, A spring, a spring, a marvelous thing, everyone knows, it's Slinky, It gives a big lift, when wrapped as a gift, a very likeable toy, It's falling in place brings smiles to your face, something kids can enjoy, It's Slinky, it's Slinky, it's fun for a wonderful toy, It's Slinky, it's Slinky, it's fun for a girl and a boy, There's Slinkymobiles with big Slinky wheels and pistons that move as you go, It makes a great sound when you pull it around, the driver's an old-timing fellow, A Slinky dog a Slinky train, many more wonderful toys, You tug their string, they do their thing, they're great for girls and boys, They're Slinky's, they're Slinky's, really wonderful toys, They're Slinky's, they're Slinky's, they're fun for girls and boys.

ACKNOWLEDGEMENTS

The copyrights of the images and text in Rose Colored: 50s are owned by the following individuals or organizations who have granted the publisher the right to use them. Every effort has been made to trace the copyright holders and the publisher apologizes for any unintentional omission. We would be pleased to hear from any not acknowledged here and undertake to make all reasonable efforts to include the appropriate acknowledgement in any subsequent editions.

MATTEL, BARBIE and associated trademarks and trade dress are owned by and used with permission from Mattel, Inc. © 2004 Mattel, Inc. All Rights Reserved.; Brylcreem® and A Little Dab'll Do Ya!® are registered trademarks of J.B. Williams Company, Inc., used under license from Combe Incorporated; "Rock Around the Clock" used with permission from Sony/ATV Music Publishing on behalf of Myers Music Inc.; Seven Year Itch photos from Getty Images; Hoover © advertisement permission from The Hoover Company, North Canton, Ohio; Roger Bannister Sports Illustrated cover © Mark Kauffman/SPORTS ILLUSTRATED; American Bandstand® images from Getty Images; Howdy Doody TM images from Getty Images; Lassie TM images from Getty Images; Captain Kangaroo TM images from Getty Images; The Mickey Mouse Club TM images from Getty Images; Pulp Fiction images © 1995-2004 Jeffrey Luther/PC Design, www.pulpcards.com. All Rights Reserved; I Love Lucy TM images from Getty Images; Janet and John TM & © The Contender Entertainment Group 2004; Dick and Jane is used with permission from Pearson Education Group; Buddy Holly images from Getty Images; Diners Club courtesy of Citicorp Diners Club Inc.; Davy Crockett images from Getty Images; "The Ballad of Davy Crockett" permission from Walt Disney Music Publishing; Ben Hur images from Getty Images; Dr. Seuss and the cover from The Cat In The Hat permission from Random House, Inc.; Eloise film still from Playhouse 90, courtesy of CBS Broadcasting Inc.; Eloise book image from Getty Images; Cinerama and the accordion logo registered trademarks of Cinerama Inc. Used with permission; The Ed Sullivan Show TM images from Getty Images; The Tonight Show TM images from Getty Images; The Jack Paar Tonight Show TM images from Getty Images; A Streetcar Named Desire TM images from Getty Images On the WaterfrontTM images from Getty Images; Bobby Soxers "Cheerleaders watch boy do routine" © Jack Moebes/CORBIS; Forbidden Planet TM images from bfi; Olympics images and logo: © IOC/Olympic Museum Collections; MAD Magazine #1 © 1952, MAD Magazine #4 © 1953 & MAD Magazine #11 © 1954 EC Publications, Inc. Used with permission. All rights reserved; Beetle Bailey © 2004 King Features Syndicate Inc./Hearst Holdings, reproduced with kind permission; Peanuts © IPL/United Media; Ajax® jingle © Colgate-Palmolive Company; Bosco® jingle © Bosco® Products, Inc.; Slinky® advertisement and jingle © POOF®-Slinky®, Inc.

The publisher would also like to thank the following individuals and organizations for their assistance in the preparation of this book:

Ruth-Anna Hobday; Sonia Yoshioka-Carroll; Victoria Skinner; Holly Stevens; Phil and Sheryl Vautier at ICE Design; Annie Matthee; Jenny Moore; Ana Vidovich; Sean Neely; Les Krantz; Sarah McSkimming; Chris Hood; Nik Andrew; Ruth Hamilton; Candace Rich at www.fiftiesweb.com; David Hall at Ephemera Now, www.ephemeranow.com; Jim Heimann; The British Film Institute; www.EdMcBain.com; Virginian at Girdlezone www.girdlezone.org; Steven Marinovich; The Tolkien Society, www.tolkiensociety.org, founded in 1969 to further interest in the life and works of J.R.R. Tolkien, C.B.E., the author of The Hobbit, The Lord of the Rings, The Silmarillion and other works of fiction and philological study. Based in the United Kingdom and registered as an independent, non-profit making charity, number 273809, the Society has an international membership which benefits from regular publications and events. Contact: The Membership Secretary, 65 Wentworth Crescent, Ash Vale, Aldershot, Surrey, GU12 5LF, UK; Josella at Tackorama, www.anzwers.org/free/tackorama/index.html; David Massey at www.bellsystemmemorial.com; Martin Hart at www.widescreenmuseum.com; Roland Latalie at www.cinerama.topcities.com; Rich Heierling at http://home.earthlink.net/~richishere/index.html; Gus Frederick of the Wolverine Antique Music Society, www.shellac.org/wams; MAD Magazine™ covers courtesy of Doug Gilford www.collectmad.com; Sally, Dick & Jane and Alice & Jerry courtesty of Denise at TagNwag Children's Books, www.tagnwag.com.

All other images Getty Images, www.gettyimages.com.

DVD documentary produced by Les Krantz, Copyright © 2004 Wildwood Films (Div. of Facts that Matter, Inc.).

Special thanks to Michael Fragnito and Susan Lauzau.

A BARNES & NOBLE BOOK

ISBN 0-7607-5951-0

Printed and bound in China by Everbest Printing Co Ltd

1 3 5 7 9 10 8 6 4 2

ROSE COLORED

DVD Contents

This original thirty-minute documentary was specially produced as a complement to *Rose Colored 50s*. Sit back and enjoy the sights and sounds of the decade that celebrated the swell, smooth and dreamy.

Introduction

1. **Sports**
   - Ben Hogan wins the U.S. Open Golf Tournament at Merion Golf Club, East Course, in Ardmore, Pennsylvania (1950)
   - Bobby Thomson hits the home run called "the Shot Heard Round the World" off Ralph Branca in the National League playoff, New York Giants vs. the Brooklyn Dodgers, at the Polo Grounds on October 3 (1951)

2. **Marlon Brando**
   - Movie scenes from *A Streetcar Named Desire* (1951), starring Marlon Brando as Stanley Kowalski, Vivien Leigh as Blanche Dubois, and Kim Hunter as Stella Kowalski

3. **Early Television**
   - Ed Sullivan hosts *Toast of the Town* (early 1950s)
   - Lucy and Desi appear in an ad for Philip Morris and a PSA for the Heart Fund
   - Network promo for *Amos 'n' Andy*, starring Alvin Childress as Amos Jones, Spencer Williams Jr. as Andrew Hogg (Andy) Brown, and Tim Moore as George "Kingfish" Stevens (circa 1951–1953)
   - Network promo for *The Many Loves of Dobie Gillis*, starring Dwayne Hickman as Dobie Gillis and Bob Denver as Maynard G. Krebs

4. **James Dean**
   - Movie scenes from *Rebel Without a Cause* (1955), starring James Dean as Jim Stark and Natalie Wood as Judy

5. **Alan Freed**
   - Disc jockey Alan Freed highlights the origins of rock 'n' roll in *Mister Rock and Roll* (1957)

6. **Elvis Presley**
   - Promo for *Love Me Tender* showing Elvis Presley appearing before adoring fans (1956)
   - Movie scenes from *Love Me Tender*, starring Elvis Presley, Debra Paget, and Richard Egan (1956)

7. **Marilyn Monroe**
   - Press footage of Marilyn Monroe
   - Movie scenes from *Gentlemen Prefer Blondes*, starring Marilyn Monroe as Lorelei Lee, Jane Russell as Dorothy Shaw, and Charles Coburn as Sir Francis Beekman (1953)
   - Movie scenes from *The Seven Year Itch*, starring Marilyn Monroe as The Girl, Tom Ewell as Richard Sherman, and Evelyn Keyes as Helen Sherman (1955)

8. **Jayne Mansfield**
   - Press footage of Jayne Mansfield
   - Movie scenes from *The Girl Can't Help It*, starring Jayne Mansfield as Jerri Jordan, Tom Ewell as Tom Miller, Edmond O'Brien as Marty Murdock, and Julie London as herself (1956)

9. ***The Lone Ranger***
   - Television show (aired from 1949 to 1957) and movie (1956), starring Clayton Moore as The Lone Ranger and Jay Silverheels as Tonto

10. ***Davy Crockett***
    - Television show (aired 1954 to 1956) and movie (1955), starring Fess Parker as Davy Crockett and Buddy Ebsen as George Russell

11. ***South Pacific***
    - Movie scenes from the Rodgers and Hammerstein musical *South Pacific*, starring Mitzi Gaynor as Nellie Forbush, John Kerr as Joe Cable, Rossano Brazzi as Emile de Becque, and Ray Walston as Luther Billis (1958)
    - Press footage of Mitzi Gaynor, Rossano Brazzi, and other stars arriving at the world premiere of *South Pacific* (1958)

Conclusion